Glencoe Spanish 2

¡Buen viaje!

Lesson Plans

Glencoe McGraw-Hill

New York, New York   Columbus, Ohio   Woodland Hills, California   Peoria, Illinois

Glencoe/McGraw-Hill

A Division of The McGraw·Hill Companies

Copyright ©2000 by Glencoe/McGraw-Hill. All rights reserved. Except as
permitted under the United States Copyright Act, no part of this publication
may be reproduced or distributed in any form or by any means, or stored
in a database or retrieval system, without the prior permission of the publisher.

Send all inquiries to:
Glencoe/McGraw-Hill
8787 Orion Place
Columbus, OH 43240

ISBN 0-02-641565-8

Printed in the United States of America.

3 4 5 6 7 8 9 10   009   08 07 06 05 04 03 02 01 00

CONTENTS

INTRODUCTION

These Lesson Plans for Glencoe Spanish, **¡Buen viaje!** Level 2 have been developed to show how the material may be distributed over the Level 2 Spanish course in logical and progressive manner. The plans may be used as presented or they are flexible enough to allow for the teacher's own creative adaptation.

To encourage the teacher to tailor these plans to his or her personal teaching situation, there are no specific time limits placed on any teaching activity. As further encouragement, space has been provided on each day's lesson plan for the teacher to write additional and/or alternate teaching activities to those suggested.

The Lesson Plans include use of the numerous support materials comprising the **Glencoe Spanish** Level 2 teaching package. These support materials are introduced in a logical manner, depending on the nature of the presentation material on a given day. For example, the Vocabulary Transparencies and the Audiocassette/CD Program can be used most effectively when presenting the chapter vocabulary. On the other hand, the Chapter Quizzes are suggested for use one or two days following the initial presentation of vocabulary or a specific chapter grammar topic.

Teacher's Name _____ Date _____

Class(es) _____ Date(s) _____ M Tu W Th F

LOCAL OBJECTIVES	**BRR:** Bell Ringer Review **STM:** Student Tape Manual **TWE:** Teacher's Wraparound Edition **WKBK:** Workbook **CQ:** Chapter Quizzes

Note to the teacher: For all Lesson Plan activities based on the student textbook you may use the CD-ROM version of *¡Buen viaje!* The CD-ROM is also an excellent reinforcement tool for students to use on those days when the class does not meet.

FOCUS

____ TWE, BRR, p. R2. In small groups, have students develop lists of expressions that can be used to describe school activities.

____ Share TWE, BRR, p. R2 list with class and develop one list. Write on the board.

TEACH

____ TWE, Teaching Vocabulary, A–C, p. R2.

____ TWE, *Práctica A–C*, p. R3.

____ TWE, Teaching the Conversation A–B, p. R4.

____ TWE, *Después de conversar A*, p. R4.

—*end of 45-minute lesson*

____ TWE, **Learning From Photos**, p. R3.

____ TWE, **Learning From Realia**, p. R4.

—*end of 55-minute lesson*

ENRICHMENT / EXTENSION

____ TWE, Expansion, *Práctica A*, p. R3.

CLOSE

____ WKBK, *Act. A–D*, pp. R1–R3.

HOMEWORK ASSIGNMENTS	TEACHER NOTES

Teacher's Name _____ Date _____

Class(es) _____ Date(s) _____ M Tu W Th F

LOCAL OBJECTIVES	**BRR:** Bell Ringer Review **TWE:** Teacher's Wraparound Edition **CQ:** Chapter Quizzes	**STM:** Student Tape Manual **WKBK:** Workbook

FOCUS

_____ TWE, **Learning From Photos**, p. R1.

TEACH

_____ TWE, Teaching Structure, *Presente de los verbos en -ar*, A–C, p. R5.

_____ TWE, *Práctica A–B*, pp. R5-R6.

_____ TWE, Teaching Structure, *Los verbos **ir**, **dar** y **estar***, A–C, p. R6.

_____ TWE, *Práctica A–B*, p. R7.

—end of 45-minute lesson

_____ TWE, **Learning From Photos**, p. R6.

_____ TWE, **Learning From Photos**, p. R7.

—end of 55-minute lesson

CLOSE

_____ TWE, *Juego*, p. R7.

_____ WKBK, *Act. A–D*, pp. R4–R5.

HOMEWORK ASSIGNMENTS	TEACHER NOTES

¡Buen viaje! LEVEL 2 LESSON PLAN REVIEW A: DAY 3

Teacher's Name _____ Date _____

Class(es) _____ Date(s) _____ M Tu W Th F

LOCAL OBJECTIVES	**BRR:** Bell Ringer Review **STM:** Student Tape Manual **TWE:** Teacher's Wraparound Edition **WKBK:** Workbook **CQ:** Chapter Quizzes

FOCUS

____ Go over any homework assignments.

____ TWE, BRR, p. R5.

TEACH

____ Have students expand the list of school related verbs in BRR, p. R5, Then have students work in pairs to make up questions using these verbs. Students interview each other.

____ TWE, *Actividades comunicativas A–B*, p. R7.

—end of 45-minute lesson

____ Students expand list of -*ar* verbs that they remember from last year.

____ Using transparencies from Level 1, students describe them using vocabulary from this *Repaso.*

—end of 55-minute lesson

ASSESS

____ Testing Program, *Repaso A*, pp. 1–2, p. 117; Speaking Test, p. 161.

CLOSE

____ WKBK, *Act. A–C*, p. R6.

____ TWE, Writing Development, p. R7.

HOMEWORK ASSIGNMENTS	TEACHER NOTES

Teacher's Name _____ Date_____

Class(es) _____Date(s) _____ M Tu W Th F

LOCAL OBJECTIVES	
	BRR: Bell Ringer Review **STM:** Student Tape Manual **TWE:** Teacher's Wraparound Edition **WKBK:** Workbook **CQ:** Chapter Quizzes

Note to the teacher: For all Lesson Plan activities based on the student textbook you may use the CD-ROM version of ¡*Buen viaje!* The CD-ROM is also an excellent reinforcement tool for students to use on those days when the class does not meet.

FOCUS

_____ Go over any homework assignments.

_____ TWE, BRR, p. R10.

TEACH

_____ TWE, Teaching Vocabulary, A–C, p. R10.

_____ TWE, *Práctica A–B*, p. R10.

_____ TWE, Teaching the Conversation, A–C, p. R11.

_____ TWE, *Después de conversar A*, p. R11.

—*end of 45-minute lesson*

_____ TWE, **Learning From Photos**, p. R9.

—*end of 55-minute lesson*

ENRICHMENT / EXTENSION

_____ TWE, **Learning From Photos**, p. R11.

CLOSE

_____ WKBK, *Act. A–C*, pp. R7–R8.

HOMEWORK ASSIGNMENTS	TEACHER NOTES

Teacher's Name _____ Date _____

Class(es) _____ Date(s) _____ M Tu W Th F

LOCAL OBJECTIVES	**BRR:** Bell Ringer Review **TWE:** Teacher's Wraparound Edition **CQ:** Chapter Quizzes	**STM:** Student Tape Manual **WKBK:** Workbook

FOCUS

_____ Go over any homework assignments.

_____ TWE, BRR, p. R12.

TEACH

_____ Prepare a list of famous people. As the teacher gives the names, students tell where he/she is from. (*Julio Iglesias. Es de España. Es español*).

_____ Have the students tell the same information about a classmate or a teacher.

_____ TWE, Teaching Structure, *Presente del verbo **ser***, p. R12.

_____ TWE, *Práctica A–B*, p. R12.

—*end of 45-minute lesson*

_____ TWE, Writing Development, p. R12.

_____ TWE, **Learning From Realia**, p. R12.

—*end of 55-minute lesson*

CLOSE

_____ WKBK, *Act. A–B*, p. R9.

_____ Students take turns describing other students in class without giving their names. The class guesses who is being described.

HOMEWORK ASSIGNMENTS	TEACHER NOTES

Teacher's Name _____ Date _____

Class(es) _____ Date(s) _____ M Tu W Th F

LOCAL OBJECTIVES	**BRR:** Bell Ringer Review **TWE:** Teacher's Wraparound Edition **CQ:** Chapter Quizzes	**STM:** Student Tape Manual **WKBK:** Workbook

FOCUS

_____ TWE, BRR, p. R13.

TEACH

_____ TWE, Teaching Structure, *Sustantivos, artículos y adjetivos*, p. R13.

_____ TWE, **Learning From Photos**, p. R13.

_____ TWE, *Práctica A–C*, p. R14.

_____ TWE, *Actividades comunicativas A–C*, p. R15.

—*end of 45-minute lesson*

_____ Hand out pictures from magazines of famous models, sports personalities, actors/actresses, etc. Give one picture to every two students. Students stand before the class to tell who the person is and where he/she is from.

—*end of 55-minute lesson*

CLOSE

_____ WKBK, *Act. C–D*, p. R10.

	HOMEWORK ASSIGNMENTS	**TEACHER NOTES**

Teacher's Name _____ Date _____

Class(es) _____ Date(s) _____ M Tu W Th F

LOCAL OBJECTIVES	**BRR:** Bell Ringer Review **TWE:** Teacher's Wraparound Edition **CQ:** Chapter Quizzes	**STM:** Student Tape Manual **WKBK:** Workbook

FOCUS

____ Ask students to generate a list of adjectives that they remember.

TEACH

____ TWE, Recycling, p. R14.

____ TWE, Writing Development, p. R14.

____ TWE, **Learning From Photos**, p. R14.

—*end of 45-minute lesson*

____ TWE, **Learning From Photos**, p. R15.

—*end of 55-minute lesson*

ASSESS

____ Testing Program, *Repaso B*, pp. 3–4, p. 118; Speaking Test p. 162.

CLOSE

____ WKBK, *Act. A–B*, p. R10.

HOMEWORK ASSIGNMENTS	TEACHER NOTES

Teacher's Name _____ Date _____

Class(es) _____ Date(s) _____ M Tu W Th F

LOCAL OBJECTIVES	
	BRR: Bell Ringer Review **STM:** Student Tape Manual **TWE:** Teacher's Wraparound Edition **WKBK:** Workbook **CQ:** Chapter Quizzes

Note to the teacher: For all Lesson Plan activities based on the student textbook you may use the CD-ROM version of *¡Buen viaje!* The CD-ROM is also an excellent reinforcement tool for students to use on those days when the class does not meet.

FOCUS
_____ Go over any homework assignments.
_____ TWE, BRR, p. R18.

TEACH
_____ TWE, Teaching Vocabulary, A–C, p. R18.
_____ TWE, *Práctica A–B*, p. R19.
_____ TWE, Teaching the Conversation, A–B, p. R20.
_____ TWE, *Después de conversar A*, p. R20.
—*end of 45-minute lesson*
_____ TWE, **Learning From Photos**, p. R17.
_____ TWE, **Learning From Photos**, p. R19.
—*end of 55-minute lesson*

ENRICHMENT / EXPANSION
_____ TWE, **Geography Connection**, p. R20.

CLOSE
_____ TWE, *Juego*, p. R19.
_____ WKBK, *Act. A–D,* pp. R11–R12.

HOMEWORK ASSIGNMENTS	TEACHER NOTES

Teacher's Name _____ Date _____

Class(es) _____ Date(s) _____ M Tu W Th F

LOCAL OBJECTIVES	**BRR:** Bell Ringer Review **TWE:** Teacher's Wraparound Edition **CQ:** Chapter Quizzes	**STM:** Student Tape Manual **WKBK:** Workbook

FOCUS

____ Go over any homework assignments.

____ TWE, BRR, p. R21.

TEACH

____ TWE, Teaching Structure, *Presente de los verbos en* *-er* *e* *-ir*, A–C, p. R21.

____ TWE, *Práctica A–B*, p. R22.

____ TWE, Teaching Structure, *El verbo* **tener**, A–C, p. R23.

____ TWE, *Práctica A*, p. R23.

—*end of 45-minute lesson*

____ TWE, **Learning From Photos**, p. R21.

—*end of 55-minute lesson*

CLOSE

____ WKBK, *Act. A–C*, pp. R13–R14.

	HOMEWORK ASSIGNMENTS	TEACHER NOTES

Teacher's Name _____ Date _____

Class(es) _____ Date(s) _____ M Tu W Th F

LOCAL OBJECTIVES	**BRR:** Bell Ringer Review **TWE:** Teacher's Wraparound Edition **CQ:** Chapter Quizzes	**STM:** Student Tape Manual **WKBK:** Workbook

FOCUS

____ Go over any homework assignments.

____ TWE, BRR, p. R22.

TEACH

____ TWE, *Práctica B*, p. R23.

____ TWE, Teaching Structure, *Adjetivos posesivos*, A–B, p. R24.

____ TWE, *Práctica A–B*, p. R24.

—*end of 45-minute lesson*

____ TWE, Writing Development, p. R23.

____ TWE, **Learning From Realia**, p. R24.

—*end of 55-minute lesson*

ENRICHMENT / EXPANSION

____ TWE, **Geography Connection**, p. R22.

____ TWE, **Geography Connection**, p. R25.

CLOSE

____ Have students write and illustrate a short description of their home.

____ WKBK, *Act. D–H*, pp. R15–R17.

HOMEWORK ASSIGNMENTS	TEACHER NOTES

Teacher's Name _____ Date_____

Class(es) _____Date(s) _____ M Tu W Th F

LOCAL OBJECTIVES	**BRR:** Bell Ringer Review **TWE:** Teacher's Wraparound Edition **CQ:** Chapter Quizzes	**STM:** Student Tape Manual **WKBK:** Workbook

FOCUS

____ Go over any homework assignments.

____ TWE, BRR, p. 24.

TEACH

____ TWE, *Actividades comunicativas A–B*, p. R25.

—end of 45-minute lesson

____ Write a list of verbs (start with the list from *Práctica B*, TWE p. R19) on the board. Have students work in pairs to write as many associations as they can to each verb.

—end of 55-minute lesson

ASSESS

____ Testing Program, *Repaso C*, pp. 5–6, p. 119; Speaking Test p. 163.

CLOSE

____ WKBK, *Act. A–B*, p. R18.

HOMEWORK ASSIGNMENTS	TEACHER NOTES

Teacher's Name _____ Date _____

Class(es) _____ Date(s) _____ M Tu W Th F

LOCAL OBJECTIVES	
	BRR: Bell Ringer Review **STM:** Student Tape Manual **TWE:** Teacher's Wraparound Edition **WKBK:** Workbook **CQ:** Chapter Quizzes

Note to the teacher: For all Lesson Plan activities based on the student textbook you may use the CD-ROM version of *¡Buen viaje!* The CD-ROM is also an excellent reinforcement tool for students to use on those days when the class does not meet.

FOCUS

_____ Go over any homework assignments.

_____ TWE, BRR, p. R28.

TEACH

_____ TWE, Teaching Vocabulary, A–C, p. R28.

_____ TWE, *Práctica A–C*, p. R29.

_____ TWE, Teaching the Conversation, A–B, p. R30.

_____ TWE, *Después de conversar A*, p. R30.

—*end of 45-minute lesson*

_____ TWE, **Learning From Photos**, p. R27.

_____ TWE, Expansion, *Práctica A*, p. R29.

—*end of 55-minute lesson*

ENRICHMENT / EXTENSION

_____ TWE, **About the Spanish Language,** p. R30.

CLOSE

_____ WKBK, *Act. A–D*, pp. R19–R20.

HOMEWORK ASSIGNMENTS	TEACHER NOTES

Teacher's Name _____ Date _____

Class(es) _____ Date(s) _____ M Tu W Th F

LOCAL OBJECTIVES	**BRR:** Bell Ringer Review **TWE:** Teacher's Wraparound Edition **CQ:** Chapter Quizzes	**STM:** Student Tape Manual **WKBK:** Workbook

FOCUS

_____ Go over any homework assignments.

_____ TWE, BRR, p. R31.

TEACH

_____ TWE, Teaching Structure, *Verbos de cambio radical*, A–C, p. R31.

_____ TWE, *Práctica A–B*, pp. R31–R32.

_____ TWE, Teaching Structure, *Verbos como **aburrir**, **interesar** y **gustar***, p. R32.

_____ TWE, *Práctica A–B*, p. R33.

—*end of 45-minute lesson*

_____ TWE, *Práctica C*, p. R33.

_____ TWE, **Learning From Photos**, p. R31.

—*end of 55-minute lesson*

ENRICHMENT / EXTENSION

_____ TWE, Writing Development, p. R31.

CLOSE

_____ WKBK, *Act. A–F*, pp. R21–R23.

_____ TWE, *Juego*, p. R32.

HOMEWORK ASSIGNMENTS	TEACHER NOTES

Teacher's Name _____ Date _____

Class(es) _____ Date(s) _____ M Tu W Th F

LOCAL OBJECTIVES	**BRR:** Bell Ringer Review **TWE:** Teacher's Wraparound Edition **CQ:** Chapter Quizzes	**STM:** Student Tape Manual **WKBK:** Workbook

FOCUS

____ Go over any homework assignments.

____ TWE, BRR, R32.

TEACH

____ TWE, *Actividades comunicativas A–B*, p. R33.

—*end of 45-minute lesson*

____ Give students a list of other stem-changing verbs not listed on p. R31. Have students work in pairs to develop questions and then respond to each other's questions.

—*end of 55-minute lesson*

ASSESS

____ Testing Program, *Repaso D*, pp. 7–8, p. 120; Speaking Test p. 164.

CLOSE

____ TWE, *Juego*, p. R33.

____ WKBK, *Act. A–B*, p. R24.

HOMEWORK ASSIGNMENTS	**TEACHER NOTES**

Teacher's Name _____ Date _____

Class(es) _____ Date(s) _____ M Tu W Th F

| LOCAL OBJECTIVES | **BRR:** Bell Ringer Review
TWE: Teacher's Wraparound Edition
CQ: Chapter Quizzes | **STM:** Student Tape Manual
WKBK: Workbook |

Note to the teacher: For all Lesson Plan activities based on the student textbook you may use the CD-ROM version of *¡Buen viaje!* The CD-ROM is also an excellent reinforcement tool for students to use on those days when the class does not meet.

FOCUS

____ Go over any homework assignments.

____ TWE, BRR, p. R36.

TEACH

____ Discuss who has traveled by plane; where, when, etc.

____ TWE, **Learning From Photos**, p. R35.

____ TWE, Teaching Vocabulary, A–B, p. R36.

____ TWE, *Práctica A–B*, p. R37.

____ TWE, Teaching the Conversation, A–C, p. R38.

____ TWE, *Después de conversar A*, p. R38.

—*end of 45-minute lesson*

____ TWE, **Learning From Photos**, p. R37.

____ TWE, Expansion, *Práctica A*, p. R37.

—*end of 55-minute lesson*

CLOSE

____ TWE, Expansion, p. R38.

____ WKBK, *Act. A–C*, pp. R25–R26.

HOMEWORK ASSIGNMENTS	TEACHER NOTES

Teacher's Name _____ Date _____

Class(es) _____ Date(s) _____ M Tu W Th F

LOCAL OBJECTIVES	**BRR:** Bell Ringer Review **TWE:** Teacher's Wraparound Edition **CQ:** Chapter Quizzes	**STM:** Student Tape Manual **WKBK:** Workbook

FOCUS
____ Go over any homework assignments.
____ TWE, BRR, p. R37.

TEACH
____ TWE, Teaching Structure, *Presente de algunos verbos irregulares*, A-D, p. R39.
____ TWE, *Práctica A–B*, pp. R39–R40.
____ TWE, Teaching Structure, *El presente progresivo*, A–B, p. R40.
____ TWE, *Práctica A*, p. R41.

—*end of 45-minute lesson*

____ TWE, Expansion, *Práctica A*, p. R39.
____ Refer to photos, TWE pp. R37 and R38. Have the students write or tell what they observe happening in the photos.

—*end of 55-minute lesson*

CLOSE
____ WKBK, *Act. A–D*, pp. R27–R29.

HOMEWORK ASSIGNMENTS	**TEACHER NOTES**

Teacher's Name _____   Date _____

Class(es) _____ Date(s) _____ M Tu W Th F

LOCAL OBJECTIVES	**BRR:** Bell Ringer Review **TWE:** Teacher's Wraparound Edition **CQ:** Chapter Quizzes	**STM:** Student Tape Manual **WKBK:** Workbook

FOCUS

____ Go over any homework assignments.

____ TWE, BRR, p. R38.

TEACH

____ TWE, **Learning From Realia**, p. R39.

____ TWE, *Actividades comunicativas A–C*, p. R41.

—end of 45-minute lesson

____ TWE, **Learning From Photos**, p. R41.

____ Call on students to give statements describing what they are doing in class now using the progressive tense. Statements may be true or false. The other students respond appropriately. (*Estoy hablando. Sí. Estoy corriendo. No.*)

—end of 55-minute lesson

ASSESS

____ Testing Program, *Repaso E*, pp. 9–10, p. 121; Speaking Test p. 165.

CLOSE

____ WKBK, *Act. A–B*, p. R30.

HOMEWORK ASSIGNMENTS	TEACHER NOTES

Teacher's Name _____ Date _____

Class(es) _____ Date(s) _____ M Tu W Th F

LOCAL OBJECTIVES	
	BRR: Bell Ringer Review **STM:** Student Tape Manual
	TWE: Teacher's Wraparound Edition **WKBK:** Workbook
	CQ: Chapter Quizzes

Note to the teacher: For all Lesson Plan activities based on the student textbook you may use the CD-ROM version of *¡Buen viaje!* The CD-ROM is also an excellent reinforcement tool for students to use on those days when the class does not meet.

FOCUS

____ Go over any homework assignments.

____ TWE, BRR, p. R44.

TEACH

____ TWE, Teaching Vocabulary, A–B, p. R44.

____ TWE, *Práctica A–B*, p. R45.

____ TWE, Teaching the Conversation, A–B, p. R46.

____ TWE, *Después de conversar A*, p. R46.

—*end of 45-minute lesson*

____ TWE, **Learning From Photos**, p. R43.

____ TWE, **Learning From Realia**, p. R46.

—*end of 55-minute lesson*

CLOSE

____ WKBK, *Act. A–D*, pp. R31–R32.

____ TWE, *Juego*, p. R45.

HOMEWORK ASSIGNMENTS	TEACHER NOTES

Teacher's Name _____ Date _____

Class(es) _____ Date(s) _____ M Tu W Th F

LOCAL OBJECTIVES	**BRR:** Bell Ringer Review **TWE:** Teacher's Wraparound Edition **CQ:** Chapter Quizzes	**STM:** Student Tape Manual **WKBK:** Workbook

FOCUS

_____ Go over any homework assignments.

_____ TWE, BRR, p. R47.

TEACH

_____ TWE, Teaching Structure, ***Ser** y **estar***, A–C, p. R47.

_____ TWE, *Práctica A–B*, pp. R47–R48.

_____ TWE, Teaching Structure, *Verbos reflexivos*, A–C, p. R48.

_____ TWE, *Práctica A–B*, p. R49.

—*end of 45-minute lesson*

_____ TWE, Writing Development, p. R48.

—*end of 55-minute lesson*

CLOSE

_____ WKBK, *Act. A–E*, pp. R33–R35.

	HOMEWORK ASSIGNMENTS	**TEACHER NOTES**

Teacher's Name _____ Date _____

Class(es) _____ Date(s) _____ M Tu W Th F

LOCAL OBJECTIVES	**BRR:** Bell Ringer Review **TWE:** Teacher's Wraparound Edition **CQ:** Chapter Quizzes	**STM:** Student Tape Manual **WKBK:** Workbook

FOCUS

_____ Go over any homework assignments.

_____ TWE, BRR, p. R48.

TEACH

_____ TWE, *Actividades comunicativas A–B*, p. R49.

—*end of 45-minute lesson*

_____ Have students brainstorm a list of reflexive verbs to describe their day's activities from start to finish.

_____ Give students partial sentences that they must complete with *es* or *está*: _____ *de Colombia. (Es)* _____ *contento hoy. (Está).*

—*end of 55-minute lesson*

ASSESS

_____ Testing Program, *Repaso E*, pp. 11–12, p. 122; Speaking Test p. 166.

CLOSE

_____ WKBK, *Act. A–B*, pp. R35–R36.

HOMEWORK ASSIGNMENTS	TEACHER NOTES

Teacher's Name _____ Date _____

Class(es) _____ Date(s) _____ M Tu W Th F

LOCAL OBJECTIVES	**BRR:** Bell Ringer Review **TWE:** Teacher's Wraparound Edition **CQ:** Chapter Quizzes	**STM:** Student Tape Manual **WKBK:** Workbook

Note to the teacher: For all Lesson Plan activities based on the student textbook you may use the CD-ROM version of *¡Buen viaje!* The CD-ROM is also an excellent reinforcement tool for students to use on those days when the class does not meet.

FOCUS
____ Go over any homework assignments.
____ TWE, BRR, p. R52.

TEACH
____ TWE, Teaching Vocabulary, A–B, p. R52.
____ TWE, *Práctica A–B*, p. R53.
____ TWE, Teaching the Conversation, A–B, p. R54.
____ TWE, *Después de conversar A*, p. R54.
—*end of 45-minute lesson*
____ TWE, Expansion, *Práctica A–B*, p. R53.
—*end of 55-minute lesson*

CLOSE
____ WKBK, *Act. A–C*, pp. R37–R38.

HOMEWORK ASSIGNMENTS	TEACHER NOTES

Teacher's Name _____ Date _____

Class(es) _____ Date(s) _____ M Tu W Th F

LOCAL OBJECTIVES	**BRR:** Bell Ringer Review **STM:** Student Tape Manual
	TWE: Teacher's Wraparound Edition **WKBK:** Workbook
	CQ: Chapter Quizzes

FOCUS

_____ Go over any homework assignments.

_____ TWE, BRR, p. R55.

TEACH

_____ TWE, Teaching Structure, *El pretérito*, A–D, p. R55.

_____ TWE, *Práctica A–B*, pp. R55–R56.

_____ TWE, Teaching Structure, *Los pronombres de complemento*, A–B, R56.

_____ TWE, *Práctica A–C*, p. R57.

—end of 45-minute lesson

_____ Have students work individually to develop a set of five questions to ask what his/her partner did last weekend or last summer.

_____ Select students to report on their interviews. Do as many as time permits.

—end of 55 minute-lesson

CLOSE

_____ WKBK, *Act. A–E*, pp. R39–R41.

HOMEWORK ASSIGNMENTS	TEACHER NOTES

Teacher's Name _____ Date _____

Class(es) _____ Date(s) _____ M Tu W Th F

LOCAL OBJECTIVES	**BRR:** Bell Ringer Review **TWE:** Teacher's Wraparound Edition **CQ:** Chapter Quizzes	**STM:** Student Tape Manual **WKBK:** Workbook

FOCUS

_____ Go over any homework assignments.

TEACH

_____ TWE, Recycling, p. R54.

_____ TWE, *Actividades comunicativas A–B*, p. R57.

—*end of 45-minute lesson*

_____ TWE, **Learning From Photos**, p. R51.

_____ TWE, **Learning From Photos**, p. R53.

—*end of 55-minute lesson*

ASSESS

_____ Testing Program, *Repaso G*, pp. 13–14, p. 123; Speaking Test p. 167.

CLOSE

_____ WKBK, *Act. A–E*, pp. R41–R42.

HOMEWORK ASSIGNMENTS	TEACHER NOTES

Teacher's Name _____ Date _____

Class(es) _____ Date(s) _____ M Tu W Th F

LOCAL OBJECTIVES	
	BRR: Bell Ringer Review **STM:** Student Tape Manual **TWE:** Teacher's Wraparound Edition **WKBK:** Workbook **CQ:** Chapter Quizzes

Chapter Objectives: The students will

- use expressions related to train travel.
- purchase a train ticket and request information about arrival, departure, etc.
- talk about more past events or activities.
- tell what people say.
- discuss an interesting train trip in Spain.

Note to teacher: For all Lesson Plan activities based on the student textbook you may use the CD-ROM version of *¡Buen viaje!* The CD-ROM is also an excellent reinforcement tool for students to use on those days when the class does not meet.

FOCUS

____ Go over any homework assignments.

____ Give an overview of the chapter and explain TWE, **Chapter Projects,** p.1.

____ TWE, BRR, p. 2.

____ Write 5–10 previously learned verbs in the preterite on the board or on an overhead projector. Have the students write sentences with them relating to travel, if possible.

TEACH

____ TWE, Teaching Vocabulary, *Palabras 1*, A–D, pp. 2–3.

____ TWE, *Práctica A–C,* pp. 4–5.

____ TWE, *Actividad comunicativa A*, p. 5.

—end of 45-minute lesson

____ TWE, **Pantomime 1-2,** pp. 2–3.

____ TWE, **Learning From Photos,** p. 1.

—end of 55-minute lesson

ENRICHMENT / EXPANSION

____ TWE, **Spotlight on Culture**, p. 1.

____ TWE, **About the Spanish Language,** p. 3.

____ TWE, Writing Development, p. 4.

____ TWE, **Learning From Realia**, p. 5.

____ TWE, Technology Option, p. 5.

____ TWE, **Learning From Photos**, p. 5.

CLOSE

____ TWE, Informal Assessment, p. 3.

____ WKBK, *Act. A–B*, pp. 1–2.

Teacher's Name _____ Date _____

Class(es) _____ Date(s) _____ M Tu W Th F

LOCAL OBJECTIVES	**BRR:** Bell Ringer Review **STM:** Student Tape Manual
	TWE: Teacher's Wraparound Edition **WKBK:** Workbook
	CQ: Chapter Quizzes

Chapter Objectives: The students will

- use expressions related to train travel.
- purchase a train ticket and request information about arrival, departure, etc.
- talk about more past events or activities.
- tell what people say.
- discuss an interesting train trip in Spain.

FOCUS

____ Go over any homework assignments.

____ TWE, BRR, p. 6.

TEACH

____ TWE, Teaching Vocabulary, *Palabras 2*, A–B, p. 6.

____ TWE, *Práctica A–C*, p. 8.

____ TWE, *Actividades comunicativas A–B*, p. 9.

____ STM, *Actividades A–G*, pp. 1–6, (Cassette 2A/CD1).

—*end of 45-minute lesson*

____ TWE, **Pantomime**, p. 6.

—*end of 55-minute lesson*

ENRICHMENT / EXPANSION

____ TWE, **About the Spanish Language,** p. 7.

____ TWE, **Did You Know?**, p. 8.

____ TWE, **Geography Connection**, p. 9.

____ TWE, **Learning From Photos**, p. 9.

CLOSE

____ WKBK, *Act. C–E*, pp. 3–4.

HOMEWORK ASSIGNMENTS	**TEACHER NOTES**

Teacher's Name _____ Date _____

Class(es) _____ Date(s) _____ M Tu W Th F

LOCAL OBJECTIVES	
	BRR: Bell Ringer Review **STM:** Student Tape Manual **TWE:** Teacher's Wraparound Edition **WKBK:** Workbook **CQ:** Chapter Quizzes

Chapter Objectives: The students will

- use expressions related to train travel.
- purchase a train ticket and request information about arrival, departure, etc.
- talk about more past events or activities.
- tell what people say.
- discuss an interesting train trip in Spain.

FOCUS

_____ Go over any homework assignments.

_____ TWE, BRR, p. 10.

TEACH

_____ TWE, Teaching Structure, *Hacer, querer y venir en el pretérito*, A–D, p. 10.

_____ TWE, *Práctica A–B*, pp. 10–11.

_____ TWE, *Actividades comunicativas A–B*, p. 11.

_____ STM, *Actividades A–B*, p. 7, (Cassette 2A/CD1).

—*end of 45-minute lesson*

_____ TWE, Expansion, *Actividad comunicativa* A, p. 11.

_____ TWE, **Learning From Photos**, p. 10.

—*end of 55-minute lesson*

ENRICHMENT / EXPANSION

_____ Prepare 10–15 statements using both present and preterite forms of *hacer, querer,* and *venir.* Read them aloud for the students. Ask them to decide if the statement they hear is present or preterite tense.

CLOSE

_____ WKBK, *Act. A*, p. 5.

HOMEWORK ASSIGNMENTS	TEACHER NOTES

Teacher's Name _____ Date _____

Class(es) _____ Date(s) _____ M Tu W Th F

LOCAL OBJECTIVES	**BRR:** Bell Ringer Review **STM:** Student Tape Manual **TWE:** Teacher's Wraparound Edition **WKBK:** Workbook **CQ:** Chapter Quizzes

Chapter Objectives: The students will

- use expressions related to train travel.
- purchase a train ticket and request information about arrival, departure, etc.
- talk about more past events or activities.
- tell what people say.
- discuss an interesting train trip in Spain.

FOCUS

____ Go over any homework assignments.

____ Review the vocabulary using Vocabulary Transparencies 1.1 (A&B) and 1.2 (A&B) with Pantomime activities.

TEACH

____ TWE, Teaching Structure, *Verbos irregulares en el pretérito*, A-F, pp. 12–13.

____ TWE, *Práctica A–B*, pp. 13–14.

____ STM, *Actividades C–D*, pp. 7–8 (Cassette 2A/CD1).

—*end of 45-minute lesson*

____ Play a verb relay game at the board to review new preterite forms and those of previous verbs or to review conjugations of the irregular verbs.

—*end of 55-minute lesson*

ASSESS

____ CQ, Quizzes 1–2, pp. 1–2.

ENRICHMENT / EXPANSION

____ TWE, **Fine Art Connection**, p. 12.

____ TWE, **About the Spanish Language,** p. 12.

____ TWE, Writing Development, p. 13.

____ TWE, **History Connection**, p. 13.

____ TWE, **Learning From Realia,** p. 14.

CLOSE

____ WKBK, *Act. B–E*, pp. 6–8.

HOMEWORK ASSIGNMENTS	TEACHER NOTES

Teacher's Name _____ Date _____

Class(es) _____ Date(s) _____ M Tu W Th F

LOCAL OBJECTIVES	**BRR:** Bell Ringer Review **STM:** Student Tape Manual **TWE:** Teacher's Wraparound Edition **WKBK:** Workbook **CQ:** Chapter Quizzes
	Chapter Objectives: The students will • use expressions related to train travel. • purchase a train ticket and request information about arrival, departure, etc. • talk about more past events or activities. • tell what people say. • discuss an interesting train trip in Spain.
	FOCUS ____ Go over any homework assignments. ____ TWE, BRR, p. 12.
	TEACH ____ TWE, Teaching Structure, ***Decir*** *en el presente*, A–C, p. 14. ____ TWE, *Práctica A–B*, p. 15. ____ STM, *Actividad E*, p. 9 (Cassette 2A/CD1). *—end of 45-minute lesson* ____ Have the students imagine *desastres* which happened on a recent trip or on a bad day at school. Working together have them make a list of possibilities and present them to the class. For example: *¡Hice mi maleta pero olvidé mis calcetines!* or *Hice mi tarea, pero la olvidé en casa. Llamé a mi madre pero ella no vino a la escuela con mi tarea. ¡Recibí cero!* *—end of 55-minute lesson*
	ASSESS ____ CQ, Quiz 3, p. 3.
	ENRICHMENT / EXPANSION ____ TWE, Expansion, *Práctica A*, p. 15. ____ TWE, **Learning From Realia**, p. 15.
	CLOSE ____ WKBK, *Act. F*, p. 8.
	HOMEWORK ASSIGNMENTS **TEACHER NOTES**

LEVEL 2 LESSON PLAN CHAPTER 1: DAY 6

Teacher's Name _____ Date_____

Class(es) _____ Date(s) _____ M Tu W Th F

LOCAL OBJECTIVES	**BRR:** Bell Ringer Review **STM:** Student Tape Manual
	TWE: Teacher's Wraparound Edition **WKBK:** Workbook
	CQ: Chapter Quizzes

Chapter Objectives: The students will

- use expressions related to train travel.
- purchase a train ticket and request information about arrival, departure, etc.
- talk about more past events or activities.
- tell what people say.
- discuss an interesting train trip in Spain.

FOCUS
____ Go over any homework assignments.

____ Have students work in pairs to write riddles using the new vocabulary. For example: *Ud. lo compra cuando Ud. va y no regresa.* (*un billete sencillo*). Collect them and use as a review.

TEACH
____ TWE, Teaching the Conversation, A–E, p. 16. Use STM, *Actividades F–G*, pp. 9–10 (Cassette 2A/CD1).

____ TWE, *Actividades comunicativas A–B*, p. 7.

____ TWE, Teaching Pronunciation, A–C, p. 17, STM, *Actividad H*, p.10 (Cassette 2A/CD1).

—*end of 45-minute lesson*

____ TWE, Technology Option, p. 16.

—*end of 55-minute lesson*

ENRICHMENT / EXPANSION
____ TWE, **Learning From Photos**, p. 16.

____ TWE, Technology Option, p. 17.

CLOSE
____ STM, *Actividades A–C*, pp. 11–12 (Cassette 2A/CD1).

HOMEWORK ASSIGNMENTS	TEACHER NOTES

Teacher's Name _____ Date _____

Class(es) _____ Date(s) _____ M Tu W Th F

LOCAL OBJECTIVES	
	BRR: Bell Ringer Review **STM:** Student Tape Manual **TWE:** Teacher's Wraparound Edition **WKBK:** Workbook **CQ:** Chapter Quizzes

Chapter Objectives: The students will

- use expressions related to train travel.
- purchase a train ticket and request information about arrival, departure, etc.
- talk about more past events or activities.
- tell what people say.
- discuss an interesting train trip in Spain.

FOCUS

____ Go over any homework assignments.

____ TWE, BRR, p. 16.

TEACH

____ TWE, Teaching the Reading, *En el AVE*, pp. 18–19.

____ TWE, *Después de leer A–B* p. 19.

____ TWE, *Actividades orales A–B*, p. 24.

____ TWE, *Actividad escrita A*, p. 25.

—end of 45-minute lesson

____ Have the students summarize what they have learned in this chapter. Write this information on the board.

____ Call out statements in both present and preterite using the verbs from the chapter. Have students indicate whether the statements are present or past on a sheet.

—end of 55-minute lesson

ASSESS

____ CQ, Quizzes 4, 5, pp. 4-5.

ENRICHMENT / EXPANSION

____ TWE, Technology Option, p. 18.

____ TWE, **History Connection**, p. 19.

____ TWE, *Lectura opcional*, pp. 20-21.

____ TWE, **Video Connection,** p. 20.

____ TWE, **Learning From Photos**, p. 21.

____ TWE, Informal Assessment, p. 21.

____ TWE, Technology Option, p. 24.

CLOSE

____ WKBK, *Mi autobiografía*, p. 12.

¡Buen viaje! LEVEL 2 LESSON PLAN CHAPTER 1: DAY 8

Teacher's Name _____ Date _____

Class(es) _____ Date(s) _____ M Tu W Th F

LOCAL OBJECTIVES	**BRR:** Bell Ringer Review **TWE:** Teacher's Wraparound Edition **CQ:** Chapter Quizzes	**STM:** Student Tape Manual **WKBK:** Workbook

Chapter Objectives: The students will

- use expressions related to train travel.
- purchase a train ticket and request information about arrival, departure, etc.
- talk about more past events or activities.
- tell what people say.
- discuss an interesting train trip in Spain.

FOCUS

____ Go over any homework assignments.

____ TWE, *Tecnotur*, Video A–B, p. 27.

____ Use Vocabulary Transparencies 1.1 (A&B) and 1.2 (A&B) to review. Have students say as much as possible about the vocabulary.

____ Choose a variety of Expansion Activities Booklet activities.

—*end of 45-minute lesson*

____ Show Communication Transparency C–1 and discuss with the students.

____ Use Situation Cards, *Capítulo 1*, to practice.

—*end of 55-minute lesson*

ASSESS

____ Testing Program, *Capítulo* 1, pp. 15–18, p. 124; Speaking Test p 168; Proficiency Test pp. 189–190.

ENRICHMENT / EXPANSION

____ WKBK, *Act. A–G*, pp. 9–11.

____ TWE, *Conexiones, Las matemáticas*, pp. 22–23.

____ TWE, **About the Spanish Language,** p. 22.

CLOSE

____ TWE, Writing Strategy, A–B, p. 25.

____ TWE, Internet, p. 27.

HOMEWORK ASSIGNMENTS	TEACHER NOTES

Teacher's Name _____ Date _____

Class(es) _____ Date(s) _____ M Tu W Th F

LOCAL OBJECTIVES	**BRR:** Bell Ringer Review **STM:** Student Tape Manual **TWE:** Teacher's Wraparound Edition **WKBK:** Workbook **CQ:** Chapter Quizzes

Chapter Objectives: The students will
- order food or a beverage at a restaurant.
- identify eating utensils and dishes.
- identify more foods.
- make a reservation at a restaurant.
- talk about present and past events.
- describe some cuisines of the Hispanic world.

Note to teacher: For all Lesson Plan activities based on the student textbook you may use the CD-ROM version of *Buen viaje*. The CD-ROM is also an excellent reinforcement tool for students to use on those days when the class does not meet.

FOCUS
_____ Go over any homework assignments.

_____ Give an overview of the chapter and explain TWE, **Chapter Projects**, p. 29.

_____ TWE, BRR, p. 30.

_____ Bring a table setting to class and other useful props to use to introduce the vocabulary to the students (tablecloth, salt and pepper shakers, a bill, fake credit card, play money, etc.). Using physical actions and oral descriptions, introduce as much new vocabulary as possible.

TEACH
_____ TWE, Teaching Vocabulary, *Palabras 1*, A–C, p. 30.

_____ TWE, *Práctica A–D*, pp. 32–33.

_____ TWE, Expansion, *Práctica A*, p. 32.

_____ TWE, *Actividad comunicativa A*, p. 33.

—end of 45-minute lesson

_____ TWE, **Pantomime 1-2**, p. 30.

_____ TWE, **Additional Practice**, p. 31.

—end of 55-minute lesson

ENRICHMENT / EXPANSION
_____ TWE, **Spotlight on Culture**, p. 29.

_____ TWE, **About the Spanish Language,** p. 31.

_____ TWE, **Did You Know?**, p. 31.

_____ TWE, **Learning From Realia**, p. 32.

_____ TWE, **Learning From Realia**, p. 33.

CLOSE
_____ TWE, **Learning From Photos**, p. 29.

_____ WKBK, *Act. A–C*, pp. 13–14.

Teacher's Name _____ Date _____

Class(es) _____ Date(s) _____ M Tu W Th F

LOCAL OBJECTIVES	
	BRR: Bell Ringer Review **STM:** Student Tape Manual **TWE:** Teacher's Wraparound Edition **WKBK:** Workbook **CQ:** Chapter Quizzes

Chapter Objectives: The students will

- order food or a beverage at a restaurant.
- identify eating utensils and dishes.
- identify more foods.
- make a reservation at a restaurant.
- talk about present and past events.
- describe some cuisines of the Hispanic world.

FOCUS

____ Go over any homework assignments.

____ TWE, BRR, p. 34.

TEACH

____ TWE, Teaching Vocabulary, *Palabras 2*, A–C, p. 34.

____ TWE, **Vocabulary Expansion,** p. 35.

____ TWE, **Pantomime**, pp. 34–35.

____ TWE, *Práctica A–C*, pp. 36–37.

____ TWE, *Actividades comunicativas A–B*, p. 37.

—*end of 45-minute lesson*

____ Prepare several statements that could occur at a restaurant and have the students decide who is speaking: the customer, the server, or the cook. For example: *El menú, por favor. (el cliente) ¿Cómo le gusta el biftec, señor? (el mesero).*

—*end of 55-minute lesson*

ENRICHMENT / EXPANSION

____ TWE, **Learning From Photos**, p. 36.

____ Tape a cooking show on the Spanish channel and show it to the class.

____ Plan a field trip to a local ethnic restaurant.

CLOSE

____ WKBK, *Act. D–F*, pp. 15–16.

	HOMEWORK ASSIGNMENTS	TEACHER NOTES

Teacher's Name _____ Date _____

Class(es) _____ Date(s) _____ M Tu W Th F

LOCAL OBJECTIVES	**BRR:** Bell Ringer Review **STM:** Student Tape Manual

TWE: Teacher's Wraparound Edition **WKBK:** Workbook
CQ: Chapter Quizzes

Chapter Objectives: The students will

- order food or a beverage at a restaurant.
- identify eating utensils and dishes.
- identify more foods.
- make a reservation at a restaurant.
- talk about present and past events.
- describe some cuisines of the Hispanic world.

FOCUS

____ Go over any homework assignments.

____ Use Vocabulary Transparencies 2.1 (A&B) and 2.2 (A&B) to review. Have students say as much as possible about the vocabulary.

TEACH

____ STM, *Actividades A–H*, pp.13–18 (Cassette 2B/CD2)

____ TWE, **For the Younger Student**, p. 31.

—*end of 45-minute lesson*

____ TWE, **About the Spanish Language,** p. 35.

—*end of 55-minute lesson*

ASSESS

____ CQ, Quizzes 1, 2, pp. 6–8.

ENRICHMENT / EXPANSION

____ TWE, Writing Development, p. 32.

CLOSE

____ Have the students bring magazine pictures of various foods or eating establishments. They can create large flashcards to use with the unit.

HOMEWORK ASSIGNMENTS	**TEACHER NOTES**

Teacher's Name _____ Date _____

Class(es) _____ Date(s) _____ M Tu W Th F

LOCAL OBJECTIVES	**BRR:** Bell Ringer Review	**STM:** Student Tape Manual
	TWE: Teacher's Wraparound Edition	**WKBK:** Workbook
	CQ: Chapter Quizzes	

	Chapter Objectives: The students will
	• order food or a beverage at a restaurant.
	• identify eating utensils and dishes.
	• identify more foods.
	• make a reservation at a restaurant.
	• talk about present and past events.
	• describe some cuisines of the Hispanic world.

	FOCUS
	_____ Go over any homework assignments.
	_____ TWE, BRR, p. 38.

	TEACH
	_____ TWE, Teaching Structure, *Verbos con el cambio e → i en el presente*, A–C, p. 38.
	_____ TWE, *Práctica A–D*, pp. 38–39.
	_____ TWE, *Actividad comunicativa A*, p. 39.
	_____ TWE, Teaching Structure, *Verbos con el cambio e → i, o → u en el pretérito*, A, p. 40.
	_____ TWE, *Práctica*, A–B, pp. 40–41.
	—end of 45-minute lesson
	_____ Have students create a preference survey of their most and least favorite foods, restaurants, things to do, places to go, etc. They will then interview 5 people in the class and report their results to the class.
	—end of 55-minute lesson

	ENRICHMENT / EXPANSION
	_____ TWE, Technology Option, p. 39.
	_____ TWE, **Learning From Photos**, p. 41.

	CLOSE
	_____ TWE, Expansion, *Práctica A*, p. 40.
	_____ WKBK, *Act. A–E*, pp. 17–18.

	HOMEWORK ASSIGNMENTS	**TEACHER NOTES**

Teacher's Name _____ Date _____

Class(es) _____Date(s) _____ M Tu W Th F

LOCAL OBJECTIVES	
	BRR: Bell Ringer Review **STM:** Student Tape Manual **TWE:** Teacher's Wraparound Edition **WKBK:** Workbook **CQ:** Chapter Quizzes

Chapter Objectives: The students will

- order food or a beverage at a restaurant.
- identify eating utensils and dishes.
- identify more foods.
- make a reservation at a restaurant.
- talk about present and past events.
- describe some cuisines of the Hispanic world.

FOCUS

_____ Go over any homework assignments.

_____ TWE, BRR, p. 40.

TEACH

_____ TWE, *Actividad comunicativa A*, p. 41.

_____ STM, *Actividades A–B*, pp. 18–19 (Cassette 2B/CD2).

_____ TWE, Teaching the Conversation, A–D, p. 42. Use STM, *Actividades C–D*, pp. 20 (Cassette 2B/CD2).

_____ TWE, *Actividad comunicativa A*, p. 43.

_____ TWE, Teaching Pronunciation, A–C, p. 43. Use STM, *Actividad E*, p. 21 (Cassette 2B/CD2) and Pronunciation Transparency P–2.

—*end of 45-minute lesson*

_____ TWE, Technology Option, p. 42.

_____ TWE, *Actividad comunicativa B*, p. 43.

—*end of 55-minute lesson*

ENRICHMENT / EXPANSION

_____ TWE, Technology Options, p. 43.

_____ TWE, **Learning From Realia**, p. 43.

CLOSE

_____ WKBK, *Mi autobiografía*, p. 22.

HOMEWORK ASSIGNMENTS	TEACHER NOTES

Teacher's Name _____ Date _____

Class(es) _____ Date(s) _____ M Tu W Th F

LOCAL OBJECTIVES	**BRR:** Bell Ringer Review **STM:** Student Tape Manual
	TWE: Teacher's Wraparound Edition **WKBK:** Workbook
	CQ: Chapter Quizzes

Chapter Objectives: The students will

- order food or a beverage at a restaurant.
- identify eating utensils and dishes.
- identify more foods.
- make a reservation at a restaurant.
- talk about present and past events.
- describe some cuisines of the Hispanic world.

FOCUS

____ Go over any homework assignments.

____ TWE, BRR, p. 42.

TEACH

____ STM, *Actividades A–D*, pp. 21–22, (Cassette 2B/CD2).

____ TWE, *Technotur,* Video A–B, p. 53.

____ Have the students work together or individually to create a menu for a restaurant. They must decorate it and include a description of various features of the restaurant.

—*end of 45-minute lesson*

____ Create a "listing" activity that is timed using the new verbs Have students make a list of things that could be asked, served, fried, or followed. Give a small reward to the winning pair or team listing the most related words that are logical.

____ TWE, *Lectura opcional 1*, p. 46.

—*end of 55-minute lesson*

ENRICHMENT / EXPANSION

____ Bring a Spanish menu to class and photocopy. Have the students ask prices of certain dishes and incorporate some of the descriptions in the menus they are creating.

CLOSE

____ Show Communication Transparency C–2 and discuss with the students.

HOMEWORK ASSIGNMENTS	TEACHER NOTES

Teacher's Name _____ Date _____

Class(es) _____ Date(s) _____ M Tu W Th F

LOCAL OBJECTIVES	**BRR:** Bell Ringer Review **TWE:** Teacher's Wraparound Edition **CQ:** Chapter Quizzes	**STM:** Student Tape Manual **WKBK:** Workbook

Chapter Objectives: The students will

- order food or a beverage at a restaurant.
- identify eating utensils and dishes.
- identify more foods.
- make a reservation at a restaurant.
- talk about present and past events.
- describe some cuisines of the Hispanic world.

FOCUS

____ Go over any homework assignments.

____ TWE, Pre-reading, B, p. 45.

TEACH

____ TWE, Teaching the Reading, *La comida mexicana*, p. 44.

____ TWE, *Después de leer A*, p. 45.

____ TWE, *Actividades comunicativas A–B*, p. 50.

____ TWE, *Actividad escrita A*, p. 51.

—*end of 45-minute lesson*

____ TWE, Technology Option, p. 44.

____ TWE, **Learning From Photos**, p. 44.

—*end of 55-minute lesson*

ASSESS

____ CQ, Quizzes 3, 4, pp. 9–10.

ENRICHMENT / EXPANSION

____ TWE, **Fine Art Connection**, p. 445.

____ TWE, **Learning From Photos**, p. 46.

____ TWE, **Learning From Photos**, p. 47.

____ TWE, **Geography Connection**, p. 47.

CLOSE

____ TWE, *Juego*, p. 50.

HOMEWORK ASSIGNMENTS	TEACHER NOTES

Teacher's Name _____ Date _____

Class(es) _____ Date(s) _____ M Tu W Th F

LOCAL OBJECTIVES	**BRR:** Bell Ringer Review **TWE:** Teacher's Wraparound Edition **CQ:** Chapter Quizzes	**STM:** Student Tape Manual **WKBK:** Workbook

Chapter Objectives: The students will

- order food or a beverage at a restaurant.
- identify eating utensils and dishes.
- identify more foods.
- make a reservation at a restaurant.
- talk about present and past events.
- describe some cuisines of the Hispanic world.

FOCUS

____ Go over any homework assignments.

____ Use Situation Cards, *Capítulo 2*, to practice.

____ Choose a variety of activities from the Expansion Activities Booklet.

—end of 45-minute lesson

____ TWE, *Lectura opcional 2*, p. 47.

—end of 55-minute lesson

ASSESS

____ Testing Program, *Capítulo 2*, pp. 19–22, p. 125; Speaking Test p. 169; Proficiency Test p. 191.

ENRICHMENT / EXPANSION

____ TWE, *Conexiones, Las humanidades*, pp. 48–49.

____ TWE, Technology Option, p. 50.

____ TWE, **Critical Thinking Activity**, p. 51.

____ TWE, Technology Option, p. 51.

____ WKBK, *Act. A–E*, pp. 19–21.

CLOSE

____ Play a Bingo game related to foods and utensils.

HOMEWORK ASSIGNMENTS	TEACHER NOTES

Teacher's Name _____ Date _____

Class(es) _____ Date(s) _____ M Tu W Th F

LOCAL OBJECTIVES	
	BRR: Bell Ringer Review **STM:** Student Tape Manual **TWE:** Teacher's Wraparound Edition **WKBK:** Workbook **CQ:** Chapter Quizzes

Chapter Objectives: The students will

- talk about computers, e-mail, the Internet, faxes, and telephones.
- talk about past habitual and routine actions.
- describe people and events in the past.
- make and receive telephone calls in Spanish.

Note to teacher: For all Lesson Plan activities based on the student textbook you may use the CD-ROM version of *¡Buen viaje!* The CD-ROM is also an excellent reinforcement tool for students to use on those days when the class does not meet.

FOCUS

____ Go over any homework assignments.

____ TWE, BRR, p. 56.

____ Give an overview of the chapter and explain TWE, **Chapter Projects**, p. 55.

TEACH

____ TWE, Preview TWE, Teacher Tips, p. 57.

____ TWE, Teaching Vocabulary, *Palabras 1*, A–B, p. 56.

____ TWE, *Práctica A–C*, p. 58.

____ TWE, *Actividades comunicativas A–C*, p. 59

—end of 45-minute lesson

____ TWE, **Pantomime**, p. 56. Add additional TPR (Total Physical Response) activities using the Vocabulary Transparencies 1.1 (A&B)

—end of 55-minute lesson

ENRICHMENT / EXTENSION

____ TWE, **Spotlight on Culture**, p. 55.

____ TWE, **About the Spanish Language**, p. 57.

____ TWE, Writing Development, p. 59.

____ TWE, **About the Spanish Language**, p. 59.

CLOSE

____ STM, *Actividades A–C*, pp. 23–25 (Cassette 3A/CD-2).

____ WKBK, *Act. A–C*, p. 23.

HOMEWORK ASSIGNMENTS	TEACHER NOTES

Teacher's Name _____ Date _____

Class(es) _____ Date(s) _____ M Tu W Th F

LOCAL OBJECTIVES	**BRR:** Bell Ringer Review	**STM:** Student Tape Manual
	TWE: Teacher's Wraparound Edition	**WKBK:** Workbook
	CQ: Chapter Quizzes	

Chapter Objectives: The students will

- talk about computers, e-mail, the Internet, faxes, and telephones.
- talk about past habitual and routine actions.
- describe people and events in the past.
- make and receive telephone calls in Spanish.

FOCUS

____ Go over any homework assignments.

____ TWE, BRR, p. 60.

TEACH

____ TWE, Teaching Vocabulary, *Palabras 2*, A–C, pp. 60–61.

____ TWE, *Práctica A–C*, pp. 62-63.

____ TWE, *Actividades comunicativas A–B*, p. 63.

—*end of 45-minute lesson*

____ TWE, Writing Development, p. 62.

____ TWE, **Pantomime**, p. 60.

—*end of 55-minute lesson*

ENRICHMENT / EXTENSION

____ TWE, **Learning From Realia**, p. 60.

____ TWE, **Did you Know?**, p. 61.

____ TWE, Expansion, *Práctica A*, p. 62.

____ TWE, **Learning From Photos**, p. 63.

CLOSE

____ STM, *Actividades D–G*, pp. 26–28 (Cassette 3A/CD-2).

____ WKBK, *Act. D–G*, pp. 24–25.

HOMEWORK ASSIGNMENTS	TEACHER NOTES

Teacher's Name _____ Date _____

Class(es) _____ Date(s) _____ M Tu W Th F

LOCAL OBJECTIVES	**BRR:** Bell Ringer Review **STM:** Student Tape Manual **TWE:** Teacher's Wraparound Edition **WKBK:** Workbook **CQ:** Chapter Quizzes

Chapter Objectives: The students will

- talk about computers, e-mail, the Internet, faxes, and telephones.
- talk about past habitual and routine actions.
- describe people and events in the past.
- make and receive telephone calls in Spanish.

FOCUS

____ Go over any homework assignments.

____ TWE, BRR p. 64.

TEACH

____ TWE, Teaching Structure, *Imperfecto de los verbos en -ar*, A–D, pp. 64–65.

____ TWE, *Práctica A–C*, p. 65.

____ TWE, *Actividad comunicativa A*, p. 66.

____ TWE, Teaching Structure, *Imperfecto de los verbos en -er e -ir*, A–F, p. 66.

____ TWE, *Práctica A–C*, pp. 66–67.

—*end of 45-minute lesson*

____ Have students call out 15 to 20 -*ar* verbs and write them on the board. Students volunteer to make up questions using the verbs in the imperfect. Other students volunteer to respond.

____ TWE, *Actividad comunicativa A*, p. 68.

—*end of 55-minute lesson*

ENRICHMENT / EXPANSION

____ TWE, **Learning From Photos**, p. 64.

____ TWE, Expansion, *Práctica A–C*, p. 65.

____ TWE, Writing Development, p. 67.

____ TWE, **Additional Practice**, p. 67.

____ TWE, **Geography Connection**, p. 67.

CLOSE

____ WKBK, *Act. A–B*, pp. 26–27.

HOMEWORK ASSIGNMENTS	TEACHER NOTES

Teacher's Name _____ Date _____

Class(es) _____ Date(s) _____ M Tu W Th F

LOCAL OBJECTIVES	
	BRR: Bell Ringer Review **STM:** Student Tape Manual **TWE:** Teacher's Wraparound Edition **WKBK:** Workbook **CQ:** Chapter Quizzes
	Chapter Objectives: The students will • talk about computers, e-mail, the Internet, faxes, and telephones. • talk about past habitual and routine actions. • describe people and events in the past. • make and receive telephone calls in Spanish.
	FOCUS _____ Go over any homework assignments. _____ TWE, BRR, p. 68.
	TEACH _____ TWE, Teaching Structure, *Imperfecto de los verbos* **ser** *e* **ir**, A–C, p. 68. _____ TWE, *Práctica A–B,* pp. 68–69. _____ TWE, *Actividad comunicativa A,* p. 69. _____ TWE, Teaching Structure, *Usos del imperfecto,* A–B, p. 70. _____ TWE, *Práctica A–B,* p. 70. _____ TWE, *Actividad comunicativa A,* p. 71. —*end of 45-minute lesson* _____ TWE, *Actividad comunicativa B,* p. 71. _____ TWE, Technology Option, p. 71. —*end of 55-minute lesson*
	ASSESS _____ CQ, Quizzes 1, 2, pp. 11–12.
	ENRICHMENT / EXPANSION _____ TWE, **Vocabulary Expansion**, p. 69. _____ TWE, **Learning From Photos**, p. 69. _____ TWE, Writing Development, p. 70. _____ TWE, **Learning From Realia**, p. 71.
	CLOSE _____ WKBK, *Act. C–E,* pp. 27–28.
	HOMEWORK ASSIGNMENTS **TEACHER NOTES**

Teacher's Name _____ Date _____

Class(es) _____ Date(s) _____ M Tu W Th F

LOCAL OBJECTIVES	
	BRR: Bell Ringer Review **STM:** Student Tape Manual **TWE:** Teacher's Wraparound Edition **WKBK:** Workbook **CQ:** Chapter Quizzes

Chapter Objectives: The students will

- talk about computers, e-mail, the Internet, faxes, and telephones.
- talk about past habitual and routine actions.
- describe people and events in the past.
- make and receive telephone calls in Spanish.

FOCUS

____ Go over any homework assignments.

____ TWE, BRR, p. 70.

TEACH

____ STM, *Actividades A–D,* pp. 29–30 (Cassette 3A/CD-2).

____ TWE, Teaching the Conversation, A–D, p. 72. Use STM, *Actividades E-F,* p. 31 (Cassette 3A/CD-2).

____ TWE, *Después de conversar,* p. 72.

—*end of 45-minute lesson*

____ Use pre-selected magazine pictures that show actions. Have students describe them as if it were something that they used to do.

____ Ask two students to describe one of their elementary school teachers.

—*end of 55-minute lesson*

ENRICHMENT / EXPANSION

____ TWE, Technology Option, p. 72.

CLOSE

____ Have students bring in a baby or childhood picture of themselves. They will write a description of their life at the time of the photo, saying what they used to do and used to like. Post the photos and descriptions without names and have the other students try to identify each photo/description.

HOMEWORK ASSIGNMENTS	TEACHER NOTES

Teacher's Name _____ Date _____

Class(es) _____ Date(s) _____ M Tu W Th F

LOCAL OBJECTIVES	**BRR:** Bell Ringer Review **STM:** Student Tape Manual **TWE:** Teacher's Wraparound Edition **WKBK:** Workbook **CQ:** Chapter Quizzes

Chapter Objectives: The students will

- talk about computers, e-mail, the Internet, faxes, and telephones.
- talk about past habitual and routine actions.
- describe people and events in the past.
- make and receive telephone calls in Spanish.

FOCUS

____ Go over any homework assignments.

____ TWE, BRR, p. 72

TEACH

____ TWE, *Actividades comunicativas A–C*, p. 73.

____ STM, *Actividades A–D*, pp. 32–34 (Cassette 3A/CD-2).

____ TWE, *Tecnotur*, Video A–B, p. 83.

—*end of 45-minute lesson*

____ Using TWE, *Actividad comunicativa A*, p. 73, as a guide, bring in encyclopedias, newspaper clippings from microfiche, magazines or other sources for student to use as a reference when talking about their grandparents' youth. Ask questions or have students make statements about what things cost, what was available (especially technology/communication), etc.

ASSESS

____ CQ, Quizzes 3–5, pp. 13–15

ENRICHMENT / EXPANSION

____ TWE, **Learning From Realia**, p. 73.

____ Have students call you at home and leave a message on your answering machine to be graded as an oral test.

____ Have students call or e-mail each other at home to practice.

CLOSE

____ TWE, *Juego*, p. 73.

	HOMEWORK ASSIGNMENTS	TEACHER NOTES

Teacher's Name _____ Date _____

Class(es) _____ Date(s) _____ M Tu W Th F

LOCAL OBJECTIVES	
	BRR: Bell Ringer Review **STM:** Student Tape Manual **TWE:** Teacher's Wraparound Edition **WKBK:** Workbook **CQ:** Chapter Quizzes
	Chapter Objectives: The students will • talk about computers, e-mail, the Internet, faxes, and telephones. • talk about past habitual and routine actions. • describe people and events in the past. • make and receive telephone calls in Spanish.
	FOCUS _____ Go over any homework assignments. _____ TWE, BRR, p. 74.
	TEACH _____ TWE, Teaching the Reading, *Futura ingeniera*, p. 74. _____ TWE, *Después de leer A*, p. 75. _____ TWE, *Actividades orales A–C*, p. 80. _____ TWE, *Actividad escrita A*, p. 81. *—end of 45-minute lesson* _____ TWE, *Juego*, p. 80. _____ Have students respond to TWE, *Actividad escrita A*, p. 81 by computer, sending their work to your e-mail address. *—end of 55-minute lesson*
	ENRICHMENT / EXPANSION _____ TWE, **Did You Know?**, p. 74. _____ TWE, Technology Option, p. 74. _____ TWE, **Learning From Photos**, p. 75. _____ TWE, *Lectura opcional 1*, p. 76. _____ TWE, Informal Assessment, p. 76. _____ TWE, **Learning From Realia**, p. 76. _____ TWE, *Lectura opcional 2*, p. 77. _____ TWE, **Learning From Photos**, p. 77. _____ TWE, Technology Option, p. 81.
	CLOSE _____ WKBK, *Mi autobiografía*, p. 32.

HOMEWORK ASSIGNMENTS	TEACHER NOTES

Teacher's Name _____ Date _____

Class(es) _____ Date(s) _____ M Tu W Th F

LOCAL OBJECTIVES	**BRR:** Bell Ringer Review **TWE:** Teacher's Wraparound Edition **CQ:** Chapter Quizzes	**STM:** Student Tape Manual **WKBK:** Workbook

	Chapter Objectives: The students will • talk about computers, e-mail, the Internet, faxes, and telephones. • talk about past habitual and routine actions. • describe people and events in the past. • make and receive telephone calls in Spanish.

	FOCUS _____ Go over any homework assignments. _____ TWE, BRR, p. 80. _____ Review, using Communication Transparency C–3. Allow time for student questions and practice. _____ Use Situation Cards, *Capítulo 3,* as an oral evaluation, if desired. *—end of 45-minute lesson* _____ Choose a variety of activities from the Expansion Activities Booklet. *—end of 55-minute lesson*

	ASSESS _____ Testing Program, *Capítulo 3*, pp. 23–27, p. 126; Speaking Test p. 170; Proficiency Test p. 192.

	ENRICHMENT / EXPANSION _____ TWE, *Conexiones*, pp. 78–79. _____ TWE, **Learning From Photos**, p. 78. _____ TWE, **Additional Practice**, p. 79. _____ WKBK, *Act. A–E*, pp. 29–31.

	CLOSE _____ TWE, Writing Strategy, A–C, p. 81.

	HOMEWORK ASSIGNMENTS	**TEACHER NOTES**

Teacher's Name _____ Date _____

Class(es) _____ Date(s) _____ M Tu W Th F

LOCAL OBJECTIVES	**BRR:** Bell Ringer Review **STM:** Student Tape Manual **TWE:** Teacher's Wraparound Edition **WKBK:** Workbook **CQ:** Chapter Quizzes
	Chapter Objectives: The students will • shop for apparel and food in Spanish-speaking countries. • ask for the quantities and sizes they want. • find out prices. • talk about different types of past actions. • talk in general terms about what is done. • talk about shopping practices in Spanish-speaking countries.
	Note to teacher: For all Lesson Plan activities based on the student textbook you may use the CD-ROM version of *¡Buen viaje!* The CD-ROM is also an excellent reinforcement tool for students to use on those days when the class does not meet. **FOCUS** _____ Go over any homework assignments. _____ Discuss Chapter Objectives and **Chapter Projects**, TWE, p. 85. _____ TWE, BRR, p. 86.
	TEACH _____ TWE, Teaching Vocabulary, *Palabras 1*, A-F, pp. 86–87. Use STM, *Actividad A*, pp. 35–36 (Cassette 3B/CD-3). _____ TWE, **Vocabulary Expansion,** p. 86. _____ TWE, *Práctica A–D*, pp. 88–89. _____ TWE, *Actividad comunicativa A*, p. 89. *—end of 45-minute lesson* _____ TWE, **Pantomime**, p. 87. _____ TWE, Expansion, *Práctica D*, p. 89. *—end of 55-minute lesson*
	ENRICHMENT / EXPANSION _____ TWE, **Spotlight on Culture**, p. 85. _____ TWE, **About the Spanish Language,** p. 86. _____ TWE, **About the Spanish Language,** p. 87. _____ TWE, **Did You Know?**, p. 88. _____ TWE, Writing Development, p. 89. _____ TWE, Technology Option, p. 89.
	CLOSE _____ TWE, *Juego*, p. 89. _____ WKBK, *Act. A–D*, pp. 33–34.

Teacher's Name _____ Date_____

Class(es) _____Date(s) _____ M Tu W Th F

LOCAL OBJECTIVES	BRR: Bell Ringer Review STM: Student Tape Manual
	TWE: Teacher's Wraparound Edition WKBK: Workbook
	CQ: Chapter Quizzes

Chapter Objectives: The students will

- shop for apparel and food in Spanish-speaking countries.
- ask for the quantities and sizes they want.
- find out prices.
- talk about different types of past actions.
- talk in general terms about what is done.
- talk about shopping practices in Spanish-speaking countries.

FOCUS

_____ Go over any homework assignments.

_____ TWE, BRR, p. 90.

_____ Vocabulary Transparencies 4.1 (A–B). Call on students to name clothing items.

TEACH

_____ TWE, Teaching Vocabulary, *Palabras 2,* A–B, pp. 90–91. Use STM, *Actividad D,* p. 38–39 (Cassette 3B/CD-3).

_____ TWE, **Vocabulary Expansion**, p. 90.

_____ TWE, *Práctica A–D,* pp. 92–93.

_____ TWE, *Actividades comunicativas A–C,* p. 93.

—*end of 45-minute lesson*

_____ TWE, **Pantomime**, p. 91.

_____ TWE, Expansion, *Práctica B,* p. 92.

—*end of 55-minute lesson*

ENRICHMENT / EXTENSION

_____ TWE, **Did You Know?**, p. 90.

_____ TWE, **Did You Know?**, p. 91.

_____ TWE, **Learning From Photos**, p. 92.

_____ TWE, Technology Option, p. 93.

_____ TWE, **Did You Know?**, p. 93.

CLOSE

_____ WKBK, *Act. E–G,* p. 35–31.

HOMEWORK ASSIGNMENTS	TEACHER NOTES

Teacher's Name _____ Date _____

Class(es) _____ Date(s) _____ M Tu W Th F

LOCAL OBJECTIVES	**BRR:** Bell Ringer Review **STM:** Student Tape Manual

TWE: Teacher's Wraparound Edition **WKBK:** Workbook
CQ: Chapter Quizzes

Chapter Objectives: The students will

• shop for apparel and food in Spanish-speaking countries.

• ask for the quantities and sizes they want.

• find out prices.

• talk about different types of past actions.

• talk in general terms about what is done.

• talk about shopping practices in Spanish-speaking countries.

FOCUS

_____ Go over any homework assignments.

_____ TWE, BRR, p. 94.

TEACH

_____ STM, *Actividades B–C*, pp. 36–38, *E–G*, pp. 39–40, (Cassette 3B/CD-3).

_____ TWE, Teaching Structure, *El pretérito y el imperfecto*, A–C, p. 94.

_____ TWE, *Práctica A–C*, pp. 95–96.

_____ TWE, *Actividades comunicativas A–B*, p. 96.

—*end of 45-minute lesson*

_____ Use Vocabulary Transparencies 4.1 (A&B) and 4.2 (A&B). Have students talk about the clothes, stores, and food items.

—*end of 55-minute lesson*

ASSESS

_____ CQ, Quizzes 1, 2, pp. 16–17.

ENRICHMENT / EXTENSION

_____ Have the students work in pairs to develop five interview questions to find out what their partner did with his/her time. (*¿Qué hiciste el sábado? ¿Qué hacías los viernes después de las clases?*) Allow time for the students to practice their interview questions with each other.

CLOSE

_____ WKBK, *Act. A–C*, pp. 37–38.

HOMEWORK ASSIGNMENTS	TEACHER NOTES

Teacher's Name _____ Date _____

Class(es) _____ Date(s) _____ M Tu W Th F

LOCAL OBJECTIVES	**BRR:** Bell Ringer Review **TWE:** Teacher's Wraparound Edition **CQ:** Chapter Quizzes	**STM:** Student Tape Manual **WKBK:** Workbook

Chapter Objectives: The students will

- shop for apparel and food in Spanish-speaking countries.
- ask for the quantities and sizes they want.
- find out prices.
- talk about different types of past actions.
- talk in general terms about what is done.
- talk about shopping practices in Spanish-speaking countries.

FOCUS

____ Go over any homework assignments.

____ TWE, BRR, p. 97.

TEACH

____ TWE, Teaching Structure, *Dos acciones en una oración*, A–C, p. 97.

____ TWE, *Práctica A–C*, pp. 97–98.

____ TWE, *Actividad comunicativa A*, p. 98.

____ TWE, Teaching Structure, *Verbos como **querer** y **creer** en el pasado*, p. 99.

____ TWE, *Práctica A–D*, p. 99.

—*end of 45-minute lesson*

____ TWE, Expansion, *Práctica B*, p. 98.

____ TWE, Informal Assessment, p. 99.

—*end of 55-minute lesson*

ENRICHMENT / EXTENSION

____ TWE, **About the Spanish Language,** p. 98.

____ TWE, **Learning From Photos**, p. 99.

CLOSE

____ TWE, *Juego*, p. 98.

____ WKBK, *Act. D–F,* pp. 39–40.

HOMEWORK ASSIGNMENTS	TEACHER NOTES

Teacher's Name _____ Date _____

Class(es) _____ Date(s) _____ M Tu W Th F

LOCAL OBJECTIVES	**BRR:** Bell Ringer Review **STM:** Student Tape Manual

TWE: Teacher's Wraparound Edition   **WKBK:** Workbook
CQ: Chapter Quizzes

Chapter Objectives: The students will

- shop for apparel and food in Spanish-speaking countries.
- ask for the quantities and sizes they want.
- find out prices.
- talk about different types of past actions.
- talk in general terms about what is done.
- talk about shopping practices in Spanish-speaking countries.

FOCUS

_____ Go over any homework assignments.

_____ TWE, BRR, p. 99.

TEACH

_____ TWE, Teaching Structure, *La voz pasiva con se*, A–C, p. 100.

_____ TWE, *Práctica A–B*, pp. 100–101.

_____ TWE, *Actividad comunicativa A*, p. 101.

_____ TWE, Teaching the Conversation, A–D, p. 102. Use STM, *Actividades C–D*, pp. 42–43 (Cassette 3B/CD-3).

_____ TWE, *Después de conversar*, p. 102.

—end of 45-minute lesson

_____ Choose a variety of activities from the Expansion Activities Booklet.

—end of 55-minute lesson

ENRICHMENT / EXTENSION

_____ TWE, **Fine Art Connection,** p. 100.

_____ TWE, **Learning From Photos**, p. 101.

_____ TWE, Technology Option, p. 102.

_____ TWE, **About the Spanish Language**, p. 103.

CLOSE

_____ WKBK, *Act. G*, p. 41.

HOMEWORK ASSIGNMENTS	TEACHER NOTES

Teacher's Name _____ Date _____

Class(es) _____ Date(s) _____ M Tu W Th F

LOCAL OBJECTIVES	**BRR:** Bell Ringer Review **STM:** Student Tape Manual **TWE:** Teacher's Wraparound Edition **WKBK:** Workbook **CQ:** Chapter Quizzes

	Chapter Objectives: The students will • shop for apparel and food in Spanish-speaking countries. • ask for the quantities and sizes they want. • find out prices. • talk about different types of past actions. • talk in general terms about what is done. • talk about shopping practices in Spanish-speaking countries.
	FOCUS ____ Go over any homework assignments. ____ TWE, BRR, p. 102.
	TEACH ____ STM, *Actividades A–B*, pp. 41–42 and *Actividades A–C*, pp. 44–46. ____ TWE, *Tecnotur*, Video A–B, p. 113. —*end of 45-minute lesson* ____ Situation Cards, *Capítulo 4*. Have students practice with a partner. These situations may be practiced, then used as a part of formal evaluation for the chapter test. —*end of 55-minute lesson*
	ASSESS ____ CQ, Quizzes 3–5, pp. 18–21.
	ENRICHMENT / EXTENSION ____ TWE, *Lectura opcional*, pp. 106–107. ____ TWE, **Literature Connection**, p. 106. ____ TWE, Informal Assessment, p. 107. ____ TWE, **Learning From Photos**, p. 107.
	CLOSE ____ Use Communication Transparency C–4 to review.

	HOMEWORK ASSIGNMENTS	**TEACHER NOTES**

Teacher's Name _____ Date _____

Class(es) _____ Date(s) _____ M Tu W Th F

LOCAL OBJECTIVES	**BRR:** Bell Ringer Review **STM:** Student Tape Manual
	TWE: Teacher's Wraparound Edition **WKBK:** Workbook
	CQ: Chapter Quizzes

Chapter Objectives: The students will

- shop for apparel and food in Spanish-speaking countries.
- ask for the quantities and sizes they want.
- find out prices.
- talk about different types of past actions.
- talk in general terms about what is done.
- talk about shopping practices in Spanish-speaking countries.

FOCUS

____ Go over any homework assignments.

____ TWE, BRR, p. 104.

TEACH

____ TWE, *Actividades comunicativas A–C*, p. 103.

____ TWE, Teaching the Reading, *De compras*, pp. 104–105.

____ TWE, *Después de leer A–B*, p. 105.

____ TWE, *Actividades comunicativas B, D*, p. 110.

____ TWE, *Actividades escritas A–B*, p. 111.

—*end of 45-minute lesson*

____ TWE, *Actividades comunicativas A, C*, p. 110.

—*end of 55-minute lesson*

ENRICHMENT / EXTENSION

____ TWE, Writing Development, p. 103.

____ TWE, **Learning From Photos**, p. 103.

____ TWE, **Learning From Photos**, p. 104.

____ TWE, Technology Option, p. 105.

____ TWE, **Critical Thinking Activity**, p. 105.

CLOSE

____ Choose any remaining activities from the Expansion Activities Booklet.

HOMEWORK ASSIGNMENTS	TEACHER NOTES

Teacher's Name _____ Date _____

Class(es) _____ Date(s) _____ M Tu W Th F

LOCAL OBJECTIVES	**BRR:** Bell Ringer Review **STM:** Student Tape Manual

BRR: Bell Ringer Review   **STM:** Student Tape Manual
TWE: Teacher's Wraparound Edition **WKBK:** Workbook
CQ: Chapter Quizzes

Chapter Objectives: The students will

- shop for apparel and food in Spanish-speaking countries.
- ask for the quantities and sizes they want.
- find out prices.
- talk about different types of past actions.
- talk in general terms about what is done.
- talk about shopping practices in Spanish-speaking countries.

FOCUS

_____ Go over any homework assignments.

_____ Use Vocabulary Transparencies 4.1 (A&B) and 4.2 (A&B) to review. Have students say as much as possible about the vocabulary.

_____ Review Chapter Objectives, TWE, p. 84, asking students to give examples of what they have learned.

—end of 45-minute lesson

_____ TWE, Writing Strategy, A–C, p. 111.

—end of 55-minute lesson

ASSESS

_____ Testing Program, *Capítulo 4*, pp. 28–33, p. 127; Speaking Test p. 174; Proficiency Test p. 193.

ENRICHMENT / EXPANSION

_____ TWE, *Conexiones, El comercio*, pp. 108–109.

_____ TWE, **Learning From Realia**, p. 108.

_____ TWE, **Additional Practice**, p. 109.

_____ TWE, Technology Option, p. 110.

_____ WKBK, *Act. A–E*, pp. 42–43.

CLOSE

_____ WKBK, *Mi autobiografía*, p. 44.

HOMEWORK ASSIGNMENTS	**TEACHER NOTES**

Teacher's Name _____ Date _____

Class(es) _____ Date(s) _____ M Tu W Th F

LOCAL OBJECTIVES	
	BRR: Bell Ringer Review **STM:** Student Tape Manual **TWE:** Teacher's Wraparound Edition **WKBK:** Workbook **CQ:** Chapter Quizzes
	Lesson Objectives: The students will review the vocabulary and structures from *Capítulos 1–4* and use them successfully in the *Repaso* activities.

FOCUS

_____ Go over any homework assignments.

_____ TWE, Teaching the Conversation, A–B, p. 114.

TEACH

_____ TWE, *Después de conversar A,* p. 114.

_____ TWE, Teaching Structure, *El pretérito,* A–B, p. 115.

_____ TWE, *Práctica A–B,* pp. 115–116.

_____ TWE, Teaching Structure, *El imperfecto,* A–B, p. 116.

_____ TWE, *Práctica C–D,* p. 117.

—*end of 45-minute lesson*

_____ TWE, *Actividades comunicativas A–C,* p. 117.

—*end of 55-minute lesson*

ENRICHMENT / EXPANSION

_____ CD-ROM, Disc 1, *Juegos de repaso,* 1–4.

CLOSE

_____ WKBK, Self-Test 1, *Act. A–I,* pp. 45–49. Begin in class and finish as homework.

HOMEWORK ASSIGNMENTS	TEACHER NOTES

Teacher's Name _____ Date _____

Class(es) _____ Date(s) _____ M Tu W Th F

LOCAL OBJECTIVES		
	BRR: Bell Ringer Review **TWE:** Teacher's Wraparound Edition **CQ:** Chapter Quizzes	**STM:** Student Tape Manual **WKBK:** Workbook
	Lesson Objectives: The students will review the vocabulary and structures from *Capítulos 1–4* and use them successfully in the *Repaso* activities.	
	FOCUS ____ Correct WKBK, Self-Test 1, *Act. A–I*, pp. 45–49. *—end of 45-minute lesson* ____ Choose one or more Tasks from Performance Assessment, Tasks 1–4, to administer in addition to or instead of the Unit Test. *—end of 55-minute lesson*	
	ASSESS ____ Testing Program, Unit Test: Capítulos 1–4, pp. 34–36, p. 128; Speaking Test p. 172.	
	ENRICHMENT / EXPANSION ____ TWE, **Learning From Photos**, p. 114. ____ TWE, **Geography Connection**, p. 117.	
	CLOSE ____ TWE, *Vistas de Chile*, pp. 118-121.	
	HOMEWORK ASSIGNMENTS	**TEACHER NOTES**

LESSON PLANS
Copyright © Glencoe/McGraw-Hill

¡Buen viaje! Level 2 Review Chapters 1–4 57

Teacher's Name _____ Date _____

Class(es) _____ Date(s) _____ M Tu W Th F

LOCAL OBJECTIVES	**BRR:** Bell Ringer Review **STM:** Student Tape Manual **TWE:** Teacher's Wraparound Edition **WKBK:** Workbook **CQ:** Chapter Quizzes

Chapter Objectives: The students will

- talk about popular hobbies and games.
- talk about activities in the park.
- give details about location.
- talk about what will happen in the future.
- compare objects and people.
- describe your favorite pastime.
- talk about pastimes in Spanish-speaking countries.

Note to teacher: For all Lesson Plan activities based on the student textbook you may use the CD-ROM version of *¡Buen viaje!* The CD-ROM is also an excellent reinforcement tool for students to use on those days when the class does not meet.

FOCUS

_____ Go over any homework assignments.

_____ TWE, BRR, p. 124.

_____ Give an overview of the chapter and discuss TWE, **Chapter Projects**, p.123.

TEACH

_____ TWE, Teaching Vocabulary, *Palabras 1*, A–C, p. 124. Use STM, *Actividad A*, p. 47 (Cassette 4A/CD-3).

_____ TWE, **Vocabulary Expansion**, p. 124.

_____ TWE, **Vocabulary Expansion**, p. 126.

_____ TWE, *Práctica A–D*, pp. 126–127.

_____ TWE, *Actividades comunicativas A–B*, p. 127.

—end of 45-minute lesson

_____ TWE, Expansion, *Actividad comunicativa B*, p. 127.

_____ TWE, Technology Option, p. 127.

—end of 55-minute lesson

ENRICHMENT / EXPANSION

_____ TWE, **Spotlight on Culture**, p. 123.

_____ TWE, **About the Spanish Language,** p. 125.

_____ TWE, Writing Development, p. 126.

_____ TWE, **About the Spanish Language,** p. 127.

CLOSE

_____ WKBK, *Act. A–B*, pp. 50–51.

Teacher's Name _____ Date _____

Class(es) _____ Date(s) _____ M Tu W Th F

LOCAL OBJECTIVES	
	BRR: Bell Ringer Review **STM:** Student Tape Manual **TWE:** Teacher's Wraparound Edition **WKBK:** Workbook **CQ:** Chapter Quizzes
	Chapter Objectives: The students will • talk about popular hobbies and games. • talk about activities in the park. • give details about location. • talk about what will happen in the future. • compare objects and people. • describe your favorite pastime. • talk about pastimes in Spanish-speaking countries.
	FOCUS ____ Go over any homework. ____ TWE, BRR, p. 128.
	TEACH ____ TWE, Teaching Vocabulary, *Palabras 2*, A–B, p. 128. Use STM, *Actividad D*, p. 50 (Cassette 4A/CD-3). ____ TWE, *Práctica A–C*, pp. 130–131. ____ TWE, *Actividades comunicativas A–B*, p. 131. *—end of 45-minute lesson* ____ TWE, **Pantomime**, p. 128. ____ TWE, Expansion, *Práctica C*, p. 131. *—end of 55-minute lesson*
	ENRICHMENT / EXPANSION ____ TWE, **Learning From Photos**, p. 129. ____ TWE, **Did You Know?**, p. 129. ____ TWE, **About the Spanish Language,** p. 129. ____ TWE, Writing Development, p. 130. ____ TWE, Technology Option, p. 131.
	CLOSE ____ TWE, Writing Development, p. 131. ____ WKBK, *Ej. C–D*, pp. 51–52.
	HOMEWORK ASSIGNMENTS **TEACHER NOTES**

Teacher's Name _____ Date _____

Class(es) _____ Date(s) _____ M Tu W Th F

LOCAL OBJECTIVES	
	BRR: Bell Ringer Review **STM:** Student Tape Manual **TWE:** Teacher's Wraparound Edition **WKBK:** Workbook **CQ:** Chapter Quizzes

Chapter Objectives: The students will

- talk about popular hobbies and games.
- talk about activities in the park.
- give details about location.
- talk about what will happen in the future.
- compare objects and people.
- describe your favorite pastime.
- talk about pastimes in Spanish-speaking countries.

FOCUS

____ Go over any homework assignments.

____ Review Vocabulary, using Vocabulary Transparencies 5.1 (A&B) and 5.2 (A&B).

TEACH

____ STM, *Actividades B–C*, pp. 48–49, *E–F*, pp. 50–51 (Cassette 4A/CD-3).

____ TWE, Teaching Structure, *Futuro de los verbos regulares*, A–C, p. 132.

____ Write the pronouns on the board and the future ending next to them from the chart on TWE, p. 132. Make up questions in the future with as many different verbs as possible. As you ask the questions, point to the ending used. Point to the ending the students should use to respond.

____ TWE, *Práctica A–B*, p. 133.

—*end of 45-minute lesson*

____ Have students write five things they will do before the day is over. Each student reads a sentence. The class selects the future tense verb used in the statement.

____ To expand on the previous activity, have students write 5 things they definitely will not do. They can be as creative as they like. After sharing with the class, they can ask a partner if he or she will do these activities tonight as well.

—*end of 55-minute lesson*

ASSESS

____ CQ, Quizzes 1, 2, pp. 22–23.

ENRICHMENT / EXPANSION

____ TWE, **Learning From Photos**, p. 132.

____ TWE, Expansion, *Práctica A*, p. 133.

____ TWE, **History Connection**, p. 133.

CLOSE

____ WKBK, *Act. A*, p. 53.

Teacher's Name _____ Date _____

Class(es) _____ Date(s) _____ M Tu W Th F

LOCAL OBJECTIVES	BRR: Bell Ringer Review STM: Student Tape Manual
	TWE: Teacher's Wraparound Edition WKBK: Workbook
	CQ: Chapter Quizzes

Chapter Objectives: The students will

- talk about popular hobbies and games.
- talk about activities in the park.
- give details about location.
- talk about what will happen in the future.
- compare objects and people.
- describe your favorite pastime.
- talk about pastimes in Spanish-speaking countries.

FOCUS

____ Go over any homework assignments.

____ TWE, BRR, p. 132.

TEACH

____ TWE, *Práctica C–E*, p. 134.

____ TWE, *Actividades comunicativas A–B*, p. 135.

____ TWE, Teaching Structure, *Comparativo y superlativo*, A–E, p. 136.

____ TWE, *Práctica A–C*, p. 137.

—*end of 45-minute lesson*

____ STM, *Actividades A–E*, pp. 51–54 (Cassette 4A/CD-3).

—*end of 55-minute lesson*

ENRICHMENT / EXPANSION

____ TWE, Writing Development, p. 134.

____ TWE, **Learning From Photos**, p. 135.

____ TWE, **Learning From Realia**, p. 136.

CLOSE

____ WKBK, *Act. B–E*, pp. 54–56.

HOMEWORK ASSIGNMENTS	TEACHER NOTES

Teacher's Name _____ Date _____

Class(es) _____ Date(s) _____ M Tu W Th F

LOCAL OBJECTIVES	
	BRR: Bell Ringer Review **STM:** Student Tape Manual **TWE:** Teacher's Wraparound Edition **WKBK:** Workbook **CQ:** Chapter Quizzes

Chapter Objectives: The students will

- talk about popular hobbies and games.
- talk about activities in the park.
- give details about location.
- talk about what will happen in the future.
- compare objects and people.
- describe your favorite pastime.
- talk about pastimes in Spanish-speaking countries.

FOCUS

_____ Go over any homework assignments.

_____ TWE, BRR, p. 136.

TEACH

_____ TWE, Teaching the Conversation, A–C, p. 138. Use STM, *Actividades F–G*, p. 55 (Cassette 4A/CD-3).

_____ TWE, *Después de conversar*, p. 138.

_____ TWE, *Actividades comunicativas A–D*, p. 139.

—*end of 45-minute lesson*

_____ TWE, Technology Option, p. 138.

_____ TWE, Technology Option, p. 139.

—*end of 55-minute lesson*

ENRICHMENT / EXPANSION

_____ TWE, **About the Spanish Language**, p. 138.

_____ TWE, Writing Development, p. 139.

_____ TWE, **Geography Connection**, p. 139.

CLOSE

_____ WKBK, *Mi autobiografía*, p. 59.

HOMEWORK ASSIGNMENTS	TEACHER NOTES

Teacher's Name _____ Date _____

Class(es) _____ Date(s) _____ M Tu W Th F

LOCAL OBJECTIVES	**BRR:** Bell Ringer Review **STM:** Student Tape Manual
	TWE: Teacher's Wraparound Edition **WKBK:** Workbook
	CQ: Chapter Quizzes

	Chapter Objectives: The students will
	• talk about popular hobbies and games.
	• talk about activities in the park.
	• give details about location.
	• talk about what will happen in the future.
	• compare objects and people.
	• describe your favorite pastime.
	• talk about pastimes in Spanish-speaking countries.

	FOCUS
	____ Go over any homework assignments.
	____ TWE, BRR, p. 138.

	TEACH
	____ STM, *Actividades A–D*, pp. 56–58 (Cassette 4A/CD-3).
	____ Use a variety of pre-selected magazine pictures. Have students compare what they see in the pictures. Students may work in small groups with 4–6 pictures per group. Students then select the two pictures that are the prettiest, nicest, etc.
	____ Students take turns presenting one picture and stating comparisons that they see. Each group will show 2–3 pictures and make superlative statements.
	____ TWE, *Tecnotur*, Video A–B, p. 149.
	—end of 45-minute lesson
	____ Go back to the 5 things the students wrote that they would do on Day 3. Have the students say whether they did those things or not. Have them make five new predictions about this weekend.
	—end of 55-minute lesson

	ASSESS
	____ CQ, Quizzes 3, 4, pp. 24–25.

	ENRICHMENT / EXPANSION
	____ TWE, *Lectura opcional 1*, p. 142.
	____ TWE, **About the Spanish Language**, p. 142.
	____ TWE, *Lectura opcional 2*, p. 143.
	____ TWE, **About the Spanish Language**, p. 143.

	CLOSE
	____ TWE, *Actividad escrita A*, p. 147.

Teacher's Name _____ Date _____

Class(es) _____ Date(s) _____ M Tu W Th F

LOCAL OBJECTIVES	**BRR:** Bell Ringer Review **STM:** Student Tape Manual
	TWE: Teacher's Wraparound Edition **WKBK:** Workbook
	CQ: Chapter Quizzes

Chapter Objectives: The students will

- talk about popular hobbies and games.
- talk about activities in the park.
- give details about location.
- talk about what will happen in the future.
- compare objects and people.
- describe your favorite pastime.
- talk about pastimes in Spanish-speaking countries.

FOCUS

_____ Go over any homework assignments.

_____ Have students write 3 ways they will prepare for the test. (They should use the future tense.)

TEACH

_____ TWE, Teaching the Reading, *El domingo en el parque*, p. 140.

_____ TWE, *Después de leer A–C*, p. 141.

_____ TWE, *Actividades orales A–C*, p. 146.

_____ Choose a variety of activities from the Expansion Activities Booklet.

—end of 45-minute lesson

_____ TWE, Writing Development, p. 140.

_____ TWE, **Learning From Photos**, p. 141.

—end of 55-minute lesson

ENRICHMENT / EXPANSION

_____ TWE, Technology Option, p. 140.

_____ TWE, **Learning From Photos**, p.140.

_____ TWE, **History Connection**, p. 140.

_____ TWE, **Geography Connection**, p. 141.

_____ TWE, Technology Option, p. 146.

_____ TWE, Technology Option, p. 147.

_____ TWE, **About the Spanish Language,** p. 147.

CLOSE

_____ Give 2–3 minutes and have each student write 1–2 questions in the future. Students take turns asking their questions of other students. Students raise their hands to assist and correct errors, if needed.

Teacher's Name _____ Date _____

Class(es) _____ Date(s) _____ M Tu W Th F

LOCAL OBJECTIVES	**BRR:** Bell Ringer Review **TWE:** Teacher's Wraparound Edition **CQ:** Chapter Quizzes	**STM:** Student Tape Manual **WKBK:** Workbook

Chapter Objectives: The students will

- talk about popular hobbies and games.
- talk about activities in the park.
- give details about location.
- talk about what will happen in the future.
- compare objects and people.
- describe your favorite pastime.
- talk about pastimes in Spanish-speaking countries.

FOCUS

____ Go over any homework assignments.

____ TWE, BRR, p. 146.

____ TWE, Internet, p. 149.

____ Complete any remaining activities from the Expansion Activities Booklet.

—end of 45-minute lesson

____ Review, using Communication Transparency C–5.

____ Have students work in pairs using Situation Cards, *Capítulo 5*.

—end of 55-minute lesson

ASSESS

____ Testing Program, *Capítulo 5*, pp. 37–42, p. 129; Speaking Test p. 173; Proficiency Test, p. 194.

ENRICHMENT / EXPANSION

____ TWE, *Conexiones, Las bellas artes*, pp. 144–145.

____ TWE, **Learning From Photos**, p. 144.

____ TWE, **Learning From Photos**, p. 148.

____ WKBK, *Act.* A–D, pp. 56–58.

CLOSE

____ TWE, Writing Strategy, A–B, p. 147.

HOMEWORK ASSIGNMENTS	TEACHER NOTES

Teacher's Name _____ Date _____

Class(es) _____ Date(s) _____ M Tu W Th F

LOCAL OBJECTIVES	**BRR:** Bell Ringer Review **STM:** Student Tape Manual

TWE: Teacher's Wraparound Edition   **WKBK:** Workbook
CQ: Chapter Quizzes

Chapter Objectives: The students will

- check into and out of a hotel.
- ask for things they may need while at a hotel.
- talk about future events.
- refer to previously mentioned people or things.
- talk about lodging in the Hispanic world.

Note to teacher: For all Lesson Plan activities based on the student textbook you may use the CD-ROM version of ¡*Buen viaje!* The CD-ROM is also an excellent reinforcement tool for students to use on those days when the class does not meet.

FOCUS

_____ Go over any homework assignments.

_____ TWE, BRR, p. 152.

_____ Give an overview of the chapter and explain TWE, **Chapter Projects**, p. 151.

TEACH

_____ TWE, Teaching Vocabulary, *Palabras 1*, A–D, pp. 152–153. Use Vocabulary Transparencies 6.1 (A&B) to introduce and practice the new vocabulary. Students may pronounce after you or Cassette 4B/CD-4, STM *Actividad A*, p. 59.

_____ TWE, **Pantomime 1–2**, pp. 152–153.

_____ TWE, *Práctica A–D*, pp. 154–155.

_____ TWE, *Actividades comunicativas A–B*, p. 155.

—*end of 45-minute lesson*

_____ TWE, **Learning From Realia**, p. 155.

_____ TWE, Expansion, *Práctica B*, p. 154.

_____ TWE, Writing Development, p. 154.

—*end of 55-minute lesson*

ENRICHMENT

_____ TWE, **Spotlight on Culture**, p. 151.

_____ TWE, **Did You Know?**, p. 152.

_____ TWE, **About the Spanish Language**, p. 153.

_____ TWE, **Learning From Realia**, p. 155.

_____ TWE, Technology Option, p. 155.

CLOSE

_____ WKBK, *Act.* A–C, pp. 60–61.

LEVEL 2 LESSON PLAN CHAPTER 6: DAY 2

Teacher's Name _____ Date _____

Class(es) _____ Date(s) _____ M Tu W Th F

LOCAL OBJECTIVES	**BRR:** Bell Ringer Review **TWE:** Teacher's Wraparound Edition **CQ:** Chapter Quizzes	**STM:** Student Tape Manual **WKBK:** Workbook

Chapter Objectives: The students will

- check into and out of a hotel.
- ask for things they may need while at a hotel.
- talk about future events.
- refer to previously mentioned people or things.
- talk about lodging in the Hispanic world.

FOCUS

____ Go over any homework assignments.

____ TWE, BRR, p. 156.

____ Review vocabulary lesson from yesterday using Vocabulary Transparencies 6.1 (A&B).

TEACH

____ TWE, Teaching Vocabulary, *Palabras 2*, A–C, pp. 156–157. Use Vocabulary Transparencies 6.2 (A&B) to introduce and practice the new vocabulary. Students may pronounce after you or Cassette 4B/CD-4, STM *Actividad D*, p. 61.

____ TWE, *Práctica A–C*, p. 158.

____ TWE, *Actividades comunicativas A–B*, p. 159.

—end of 45-minute lesson

____ TWE, **Cooperative Learning**, p. 157.

—end of 55-minute lesson

ENRICHMENT / EXPANSION

____ TWE, **About the Spanish Language,** p. 156.

____ TWE, **Did You Know?**, p. 157.

____ TWE, **Did You Know?**, p. 158.

____ TWE, **Geography Connection**, p. 159.

CLOSE

____ TWE, **Pantomime**, p. 156.

____ WKBK, *Act. D–F*, pp. 62–63.

HOMEWORK ASSIGNMENTS	TEACHER NOTES

Teacher's Name _____ Date _____

Class(es) _____ Date(s) _____ M Tu W Th F

LOCAL OBJECTIVES	**BRR:** Bell Ringer Review **STM:** Student Tape Manual **TWE:** Teacher's Wraparound Edition **WKBK:** Workbook **CQ:** Chapter Quizzes

Chapter Objectives: The students will

- check into and out of a hotel.
- ask for things they may need while at a hotel.
- talk about future events.
- refer to previously mentioned people or things.
- talk about lodging in the Hispanic world.

FOCUS

_____ Go over any homework assignments.

_____ Give oral definitions and have the students give the correct vocabulary word. (*La persona que lleva las maletas es _____. La persona que se queda en el hotel es _____.*)

TEACH

_____ STM, *Actividades B–C*, p. 60, *E–F*, pp. 61–62 (Cassette 4B/CD-4).

_____ TWE, Teaching Structure, *Futuro de los verbos irregulares*, A B, p. 160.

_____ TWE, *Práctica A–C*, p. 161.

—*end of 45-minute lesson*

_____ TWE, Technology Option, p. 159.

—*end of 55-minute lesson*

ASSESS

_____ CQ, Quizzes 1, 2, pp. 26–27.

ENRICHMENT / EXPANSION

_____ TWE, Writing Development, p. 161.

_____ TWE, **Learning From Realia**, p. 161.

CLOSE

_____ WKBK, *Act. A–C*, p. 64.

HOMEWORK ASSIGNMENTS	TEACHER NOTES

Teacher's Name _____ Date _____

Class(es) _____ Date(s) _____ M Tu W Th F

LOCAL OBJECTIVES	**BRR:** Bell Ringer Review **TWE:** Teacher's Wraparound Edition **CQ:** Chapter Quizzes	**STM:** Student Tape Manual **WKBK:** Workbook

Chapter Objectives: The students will

- check into and out of a hotel.
- ask for things they may need while at a hotel.
- talk about future events.
- refer to previously mentioned people or things.
- talk about lodging in the Hispanic world.

FOCUS

____ Go over any homework assignments.

____ TWE, BRR, p. 160.

TEACH

____ TWE, *Práctica D-E*, p. 162.

____ TWE, *Actividades comunicativas A–B*, p. 163.

____ STM, *Actividades A–B*, pp. 62–63 (Cassette 4B/CD-4).

—*end of 45-minute lesson*

____ Have students ask the teacher questions using the verbs on the charts on TWE, p. 160. (*¿A qué hora saldremos de clase?*)

____ Review vocabulary using Vocabulary Transparencies 6.2 (A&B).

—*end of 55-minute lesson*

ENRICHMENT / EXPANSION

____ TWE, Expansion, *Práctica D*, p. 162.

____ TWE, **Learning From Photos**, p. 162.

____ TWE, **Vocabulary Expansion**, p. 162.

____ TWE, Technology Option, p. 163.

CLOSE

____ WKBK, *Act. D–E*, p. 65.

HOMEWORK ASSIGNMENTS	TEACHER NOTES

Teacher's Name _____ Date _____

Class(es) _____ Date(s) _____ M Tu W Th F

LOCAL OBJECTIVES		
	BRR: Bell Ringer Review **TWE:** Teacher's Wraparound Edition **CQ:** Chapter Quizzes	**STM:** Student Tape Manual **WKBK:** Workbook

Chapter Objectives: The students will

- check into and out of a hotel.
- ask for things they may need while at a hotel.
- talk about future events.
- refer to previously mentioned people or things.
- talk about lodging in the Hispanic world.

FOCUS

____ Go over any homework assignments.

____ TWE, BRR, p. 166.

TEACH

____ TWE, Teaching Structure, *Me lo, te lo, nos lo,* A–C, p. 163.

____ TWE, *Práctica A–E,* pp. 164–165.

____ TWE, Teaching the Conversation, A–D, p. 166. Use STM, *Actividades E–F,* pp. 64–65 (Cassette 4B/CD-4).

____ TWE, *Después de conversar,* p. 166.

—*end of 45-minute lesson*

____ TWE, **Learning From Photos**, p. 166.

____ TWE, **Learning From Realia**, p. 167.

—*end of 55-minute lesson*

ASSESS

____ CQ, Quiz 3, p. 28.

ENRICHMENT / EXPANSION

____ TWE, **History Connection**, p. 164.

____ TWE, **Learning From Realia**, p. 164.

____ TWE, **Learning From Photos**, p. 165.

CLOSE

____ WKBK, *Act. F–G,* p. 66.

HOMEWORK ASSIGNMENTS	TEACHER NOTES

Teacher's Name _____ Date _____

Class(es) _____ Date(s) _____ M Tu W Th F

LOCAL OBJECTIVES	**BRR:** Bell Ringer Review **TWE:** Teacher's Wraparound Edition **CQ:** Chapter Quizzes	**STM:** Student Tape Manual **WKBK:** Workbook
	Chapter Objectives: The students will • check into and out of a hotel. • ask for things they may need while at a hotel. • talk about future events. • refer to previously mentioned people or things. • talk about lodging in the Hispanic world.	
	FOCUS ____ Go over any homework assignments. ____ Make up a variety of questions using verbs in the future tense and have students respond to them orally.	
	TEACH ____ STM, *Actividades C–D,* pp. 63–64 (Cassette 4B/CD-4). ____ TWE, *Actividades comunicativas A–B,* p. 167. ____ Take a variety of items found in the classroom. Have each student select one or two items. Ask a student to give his/her item or items to another person. The student names the object(s) in Spanish. The student receiving the item(s) states what is being given to him/her. (Student #1: *La pluma.* Student #2: *Juan me la dio.*) *—end of 45-minute lesson* ____ TWE, *Actividad oral A,* p. 174. *—end of 55-minute lesson*	
	ASSESS ____ CQ, Quiz 4, p. 29.	
	ENRICHMENT / EXPANSION ____ TWE, *Lectura opcional 1,* p. 170. ____ TWE, **Did You Know?,** p. 170.	
	CLOSE ____ STM, *Actividades A–C,* pp. 66–70 (Cassette 4B/CD-4).	
	HOMEWORK ASSIGNMENTS	**TEACHER NOTES**

Teacher's Name _____ Date _____

Class(es) _____ Date(s) _____ M Tu W Th F

LOCAL OBJECTIVES	**BRR:** Bell Ringer Review **TWE:** Teacher's Wraparound Edition **CQ:** Chapter Quizzes	**STM:** Student Tape Manual **WKBK:** Workbook

Chapter Objectives: The students will

- check into and out of a hotel.
- ask for things they may need while at a hotel.
- talk about future events.
- refer to previously mentioned people or things.
- talk about lodging in the Hispanic world.

FOCUS

____ Go over any homework assignments.

____ TWE, BRR, p. 168.

TEACH

____ TWE, Teaching the Reading, *Los paradores de España*, pp. 168–169.

____ TWE, *Después de leer A–C*, p. 169.

____ TWE, *Actividades orales B–C*, p. 174.

—*end of 45-minute lesson*

____ Choose a variety of activities from the Expansion Activities Booklet.

—*end of 55-minute lesson*

ENRICHMENT / EXPANSION

____ TWE, **Learning From Photos**, p. 168

____ TWE, Technology Option, p. 169.

CLOSE

____ TWE, Technology Option, p. 175, to prepare for Writing Strategy.

HOMEWORK ASSIGNMENTS	TEACHER NOTES

Teacher's Name _____ Date _____

Class(es) _____ Date(s) _____ M Tu W Th F

LOCAL OBJECTIVES	**BRR:** Bell Ringer Review **TWE:** Teacher's Wraparound Edition **CQ:** Chapter Quizzes	**STM:** Student Tape Manual **WKBK:** Workbook

Chapter Objectives: The students will

- check into and out of a hotel.
- ask for things you may need while at a hotel.
- talk about future events.
- refer to previously mentioned people or things.
- talk about lodging in the Hispanic world.

FOCUS

____ Go over any homework assignments.

____ Use Communication Transparency C-6 to review.

TEACH

____ TWE, *Actividades escritas A–B*, p. 175.

____ TWE, *Tecnotur*, Video A–B, p. 177.

—*end of 45-minute lesson*

____ Complete any remaining Expansion Activities Booklet activities.

—*end of 55-minute lesson*

ENRICHMENT / EXPANSION

____ TWE, *Lectura opcional 2*, p. 171.

____ TWE, **History Connection**, p. 171.

____ TWE, **Geography Connection**, p. 174.

____ TWE, **History Connection**, p. 175.

CLOSE

____ TWE, Writing Strategy, p. 175.

HOMEWORK ASSIGNMENTS	TEACHER NOTES

Teacher's Name _____ Date _____

Class(es) _____ Date(s) _____ M Tu W Th F

LOCAL OBJECTIVES	
	BRR: Bell Ringer Review **STM:** Student Tape Manual **TWE:** Teacher's Wraparound Edition **WKBK:** Workbook **CQ:** Chapter Quizzes
	Chapter Objectives: The students will • check into and out of a hotel. • ask for things they may need while at a hotel. • talk about future events. • refer to previously mentioned people or things. • talk about lodging in the Hispanic world.
	FOCUS ____ Communication Transparency C–6. ____ Situation Cards, *Capítulo 6,* may be used for speaking evaluation. —*end of 45-minute lesson* ____ WKBK, *Act. A–F,* pp. 67–69. —*end of 55-minute lesson*
	ASSESS ____ Testing Program, *Capítulo 6,* pp. 43–47, p. 130; Speaking Test p. 174; Proficiency Test, p. 195.
	ENRICHMENT / EXPANSION ____ TWE, *Conexiones, La educación física,* pp. 172–173. ____ TWE, **Learning From Realia,** p. 172. ____ TWE, **Learning From Realia,** p. 173.
	CLOSE ____ WKBK, *Mi autobiografía,* p. 70.
	HOMEWORK ASSIGNMENTS **TEACHER NOTES**

Teacher's Name _____ Date _____

Class(es) _____ Date(s) _____ M Tu W Th F

LOCAL OBJECTIVES	**BRR:** Bell Ringer Review **TWE:** Teacher's Wraparound Edition **CQ:** Chapter Quizzes	**STM:** Student Tape Manual **WKBK:** Workbook

Chapter Objectives: The students will

- talk about air travel.
- discuss the influence of geography on travel in Latin America.
- talk about things that would happen under certain conditions.
- talk about air travel in Hispanic countries.

Note to teacher: For all Lesson Plan activities based on the student textbook you may use the CD-ROM version of *¡Buen viaje!* The CD-ROM is also an excellent reinforcement tool for students to use on those days when the class does not meet.

FOCUS

____ Go over any homework assignments.

____ Give an overview of the chapter and explain TWE, **Chapter Projects**, p. 179.

____ TWE, BRR, p. 180.

TEACH

____ TWE, Teaching Vocabulary, *Palabras 1*, A–D, p. 180. Show Vocabulary Transparencies 7.1 (A&B) as you introduce and practice the new vocabulary. You may also use STM, *Actividad A*, p. 71 (Cassette 5A/CD-4).

____ TWE, *Práctica A–D*, pp. 182-183.

____ TWE, *Actividades comunicativas A–B*, p. 183.

—*end of 45-minute lesson*

____ Students work in small groups to make up original sentences with the vocabulary. (*No me gusta sentarme cerca de la ventanilla. Los asientos en los aviones son cómodos.*)

____ Students share their answers orally. Students may also make incorrect statements and have the class correct them. (Student: *Podemos abrir la ventanilla.* Class: *No podemos abrir la ventanilla.*)

—*end of 55-minute lesson*

ENRICHMENT / EXPANSION

____ TWE, **Spotlight on Culture**, p. 179.

____ TWE, **Vocabulary Expansion**, p. 181.

____ TWE, **Learning From Photos**, p. 183.

____ TWE, **Did You Know?**, p. 183.

CLOSE

____ WKBK, *Act. A–C*, pp. 71–72.

Teacher's Name _____ Date _____

Class(es) _____ Date(s) _____ M Tu W Th F

LOCAL OBJECTIVES	
	BRR: Bell Ringer Review **STM:** Student Tape Manual **TWE:** Teacher's Wraparound Edition **WKBK:** Workbook **CQ:** Chapter Quizzes

Chapter Objectives: The students will

- talk about air travel.

- discuss the influence of geography on travel in Latin America.

- talk about things that would happen under certain conditions.

- talk about air travel in Hispanic countries.

FOCUS

_____ Go over any homework assignments.

_____ TWE, BRR, p. 184.

TEACH

_____ TWE, Teaching Vocabulary, *Palabras 2*, A–C, pp. 184–185. Show Vocabulary Transparencies 7.2 (A&B) as you introduce and practice the new vocabulary. You may also want to use STM, *Actividad D*, p. 73. (Cassette 5A/CD-4).

_____ TWE, *Práctica A–D*, pp. 186–187.

_____ TWE, *Actividades comunicativas A–B*, p. 187.

—end of 45-minute lesson

_____ Make up questions using the vocabulary from the BRR, p. 184. (*¿Es buena la comida que sirven en los vuelos? ¿Te gusta el asiento cerca del pasillo o cerca de la ventanilla?*)

_____ Students choose 5 vocabulary words from *Palabras 2* and write an original sentence for each. Call on students to write their sentences on the board leaving out the vocabulary word. The class tries to identify the correct vocabulary word.

—end of 55-minute lesson

ENRICHMENT / EXPANSION

_____ TWE, **Did You Know?**, p. 184.

_____ TWE, **About the Spanish Language**, p. 185.

_____ TWE, **Did You Know?**, p. 186.

CLOSE

_____ WKBK, *Act. D–G*, pp. 73–74.

HOMEWORK ASSIGNMENTS	TEACHER NOTES

Teacher's Name _____ Date _____

Class(es) _____ Date(s) _____ M Tu W Th F

LOCAL OBJECTIVES	**BRR:** Bell Ringer Review **STM:** Student Tape Manual

TWE: Teacher's Wraparound Edition **WKBK:** Workbook
CQ: Chapter Quizzes

Chapter Objectives: The students will

- talk about air travel.
- discuss the influence of geography on travel in Latin America.
- talk about things that would happen under certain conditions.
- talk about air travel in Hispanic countries.

FOCUS

_____ Go over any homework assignments.

_____ TWE, **Additional Practice**, p. 181.

TEACH

_____ STM, *Actividades B–C*, p. 72, *E–F*, pp. 73–74 (Cassette 5A/CD-4).

_____ TWE, **Pantomime**, p. 180

_____ Make photocopies of various pictures related to plane travel. Have students work in groups of 3–4 to make up questions about what is happening in the pictures. Each student should ask one question of the other students in the group and each should respond to a question at least once.

—end of 45-minute lesson

_____ Use Vocabulary Transparencies 7.1 (A&B) and 7.2 (A&B). Call students to the overhead. Do TPR. (*Toquen el aeropuerto. Hagan un círculo alrededor del helicóptero. Cubran el lago con su dedo gordo.*)

—end of 55-minute lesson

ASSESS

_____ CQ, Quizzes 1, 2, pp. 30–31.

ENRICHMENT / EXPANSION

_____ TWE, Technology Option, p. 187.

_____ TWE, **Critical Thinking Activity**, p. 187.

_____ TWE, **Learning From Photos**, p. 187.

CLOSE

_____ Review future tense, asking students what they will do tomorrow.

HOMEWORK ASSIGNMENTS	TEACHER NOTES

Teacher's Name _____ Date _____

Class(es) _____ Date(s) _____ M Tu W Th F

LOCAL OBJECTIVES	**BRR:** Bell Ringer Review **TWE:** Teacher's Wraparound Edition **CQ:** Chapter Quizzes	**STM:** Student Tape Manual **WKBK:** Workbook

Chapter Objectives: The students will

- talk about air travel.
- discuss the influence of geography on travel in Latin America.
- talk about things that would happen under certain conditions.
- talk about air travel in Hispanic countries.

FOCUS

_____ Go over any homework assignments.

_____ TWE, BRR, p. 188.

TEACH

_____ TWE, Teaching Structure, *Modo potencial o condicional de verbos regulares,* A–C, p. 188.

_____ TWE, *Práctica A–D,* pp. 189–190.

_____ TWE, Teaching Structure, *Modo potencial de verbos irregulares,* p. 191.

_____ TWE, *Práctica A–D,* pp. 191–192.

—end of 45-minute lesson

_____ TWE, **Learning From Photos**, p. 188.

_____ Write the subject pronouns and endings for the conditional on the board. Ask several questions using the conditional tense. Point to the ending on the board as you ask the question. Point to the ending that the student should use to respond.

—end of 55-minute lesson

ENRICHMENT / EXPANSION

_____ TWE, Expansion, *Práctica B,* p. 189.

_____ TWE, **Learning From Realia**, p. 190.

_____ TWE, **Learning From Photos**, p. 190.

_____ TWE, Expansion, *Práctica D,* p. 192.

CLOSE

_____ WKBK, *Act. A–D,* pp. 75–76.

_____ TWE, **Learning From Photos**, p. 189.

HOMEWORK ASSIGNMENTS	TEACHER NOTES

Teacher's Name _____ Date_____

Class(es) _____Date(s) _____ M Tu W Th F

LOCAL OBJECTIVES	**BRR:** Bell Ringer Review **STM:** Student Tape Manual **TWE:** Teacher's Wraparound Edition **WKBK:** Workbook **CQ:** Chapter Quizzes	

Chapter Objectives: The students will

- talk about air travel.
- discuss the influence of geography on travel in Latin America.
- talk about things that would happen under certain conditions.
- talk about air travel in Hispanic countries.

FOCUS

_____ Go over any homework assignments.

_____ TWE, BRR, p. 191.

TEACH

_____ TWE, *Actividades comunicativas A–B*, p. 193.

_____ STM, *Actividades A–C*, pp. 74–75 (Cassette 5A/CD-4).

_____ TWE, Teaching Structure, *Dos complementos con se*, A–B, p. 193.

_____ TWE, *Práctica A–D*, pp. 194–195.

_____ TWE, *Actividad comunicativa A*, p. 195.

—end of 45-minute lesson

_____ STM, *Actividades D-E*, pp. 76–77 (Cassette 5A/CD-4).

_____ Choose a variety of activities from the Expansion Activities Booklet.

—end of 55-minute lesson

ENRICHMENT / EXPANSION

_____ TWE, **Geography Connection**, p. 193.

_____ TWE, **Learning From Photos**, p. 194.

_____ TWE, Technology Option, p. 195.

_____ TWE, **Learning From Photos**, p. 195.

CLOSE

_____ WKBK, *Act. E–G*, p. 77.

HOMEWORK ASSIGNMENTS	TEACHER NOTES

Teacher's Name _____ Date _____

Class(es) _____ Date(s) _____ M Tu W Th F

LOCAL OBJECTIVES		
	BRR: Bell Ringer Review	**STM:** Student Tape Manual
	TWE: Teacher's Wraparound Edition	**WKBK:** Workbook
	CQ: Chapter Quizzes	

Chapter Objectives: The students will

- talk about air travel.
- discuss the influence of geography on travel in Latin America.
- talk about things that would happen under certain conditions.
- talk about air travel in Hispanic countries.

FOCUS

____ Go over any homework assignments.

____ TWE, BRR, p. 193.

TEACH

____ TWE, Teaching the Conversation, A–F, p. 196. Use Cassette 5A/CD-4 and STM, *Actividades F–G*, pp. 77–78.

____ TWE, *Después de conversar*, p. 196.

____ STM, *Actividades A–C*, pp. 79–81 (Cassette 5A/CD-4)

—end of 45-minute lesson

____ Ask the students questions and have them answer with double object pronuns. (*¿Compras el disco para Juan? Sí, se lo compro. ¿Compras las botas para tu papá? Sí, se las compro.*)

____ Collect several classroom items. Select an item and show it to the class. The class will name the item. Hand an item or items to a student or students and call on another student to state what you did. (*El lápiz. Se lo dio a Juan. Las plumas: Se las dio a Jorge y Marta.*)

—end of 55-minute lesson

ASSESS

____ CQ, Quizzes 3, 4, pp. 32–33.

ENRICHMENT / EXPANSION

____ TWE, Technology Option, p. 196.

____ TWE, **Did You Know?**, p. 197.

____ TWE, **Learning From Photos**, p. 197.

CLOSE

____ Have the students write a paragraph of 8–12 sentences. *Si you tuviera un millón de dólares, yo _____ compararía, iría, visitaría...*Finish for homework.

HOMEWORK ASSIGNMENTS	TEACHER NOTES

Teacher's Name _____ Date _____

Class(es) _____ Date(s) _____ M Tu W Th F

LOCAL OBJECTIVES	**BRR:** Bell Ringer Review **STM:** Student Tape Manual **TWE:** Teacher's Wraparound Edition **WKBK:** Workbook **CQ:** Chapter Quizzes

	Chapter Objectives: The students will
	• talk about air travel.
	• discuss the influence of geography on travel in Latin America.
	• talk about things that would happen under certain conditions.
	• talk about air travel in Hispanic countries.

	FOCUS
	____ Go over any homework assignments.
	____ TWE, BRR, p. 196.

	TEACH
	____ TWE, Teaching the Reading, *El aeropuerto que se llama «El Alto»*, pp. 198–199.
	____ TWE, *Después de leer A–B*, p. 199.
	____ TWE, *Tecnotur*, Video A–B, p. 207.
	—*end of 45-minute lesson*
	____ TWE, BRR, p. 198.
	____ TWE, **Learning From Photos**, p. 197.
	—*end of 55-minute lesson*

	ASSESS
	____ CQ, Quiz 5, p. 34.

	ENRICHMENT / EXPANSION
	____ TWE, **Critical Thinking Activity**, p. 198.
	____ TWE, **Geography Connection**, p. 198.
	____ TWE, Writing Development, p. 199.
	____ TWE, Technology Option, p. 199.
	____ TWE, **Learning From Photos**, p. 199.
	____ TWE, *Lectura opcional 1*, p. 200.
	____ TWE, **Learning From Photos**, p. 200.
	____ TWE, *Lectura opcional 2*, p. 201.
	____ TWE, **History Connection**, p. 201.
	____ TWE, **Cooperative Learning**, p. 201.

	CLOSE
	____ Choose a variety of activities from the Expansion Activities Booklet.

Teacher's Name _____ Date _____

Class(es) _____ Date(s) _____ M Tu W Th F

LOCAL OBJECTIVES	
	BRR: Bell Ringer Review **STM:** Student Tape Manual **TWE:** Teacher's Wraparound Edition **WKBK:** Workbook **CQ:** Chapter Quizzes

Chapter Objectives: The students will

- talk about air travel.
- discuss the influence of geography on travel in Latin America.
- talk about things that would happen under certain conditions.
- talk about air travel in Hispanic countries.

FOCUS

_____ Go over any homework assignments.

_____ Review using Vocabulary Transparencies 7.1 (A&B) and 7.2 (A&B).

TEACH

_____ TWE, *Actividades orales A–C*, p. 204.

_____ TWE, *Actividades escritas A–B*, p. 205.

—end of 45-minute lesson

_____ TWE, Writing Strategy, A–B, p. 205.

—end of 55-minute lesson

ENRICHMENT / EXPANSION

_____ TWE, Technology Option, p. 204.

_____ TWE, **Geography Connection**, p. 204.

_____ TWE, Technology Option, p. 205.

_____ TWE, **Learning From Realia**, p. 205.

CLOSE

_____ Choose any remaining activities from the Expansion Activities Booklet.

HOMEWORK ASSIGNMENTS	TEACHER NOTES

Teacher's Name _____ Date _____

Class(es) _____ Date(s) _____ M Tu W Th F

LOCAL OBJECTIVES	
	BRR: Bell Ringer Review **STM:** Student Tape Manual **TWE:** Teacher's Wraparound Edition **WKBK:** Workbook **CQ:** Chapter Quizzes

Chapter Objectives: The students will

- talk about air travel.
- discuss the influence of geography on travel in Latin America.
- talk about things that would happen under certain conditions.
- talk about air travel in Hispanic countries.

FOCUS

____ Go over any homework assignments.

____ Use Situation Cards to review *Capítulo 7*.

____ Show Communication Transparency C–7 and have the students describe it.

—*end of 45-minute lesson*

____ WKBK, *Act. A–E*, pp. 78–80.

—*end of 55-minute lesson*

ASSESS

____ Testing Program, *Capítulo 7*, pp. 48–52, p. 131; Speaking Test p. 175; Proficiency Test p. 196.

ENRICHMENT / EXPANSION

____ TWE, *Conexiones, Las ciencias naturales*, p. 202-203.

____ TWE, **Additional Practice**, p. 202.

____ TWE, **History Connection**, p. 202.

____ TWE, **History Connection**, p. 203.

CLOSE

____ TWE, *Mi autobiografía*. p. 81.

HOMEWORK ASSIGNMENTS	TEACHER NOTES

Teacher's Name _____ Date _____

Class(es) _____ Date(s) _____ M Tu W Th F

LOCAL OBJECTIVES	**BRR:** Bell Ringer Review	**STM:** Student Tape Manual
	TWE: Teacher's Wraparound Edition	**WKBK:** Workbook
	CQ: Chapter Quizzes	

Lesson Objectives: The students will review the vocabulary and structures from *Capítulos 5–7* and use them successfully in the *Repaso* activities.

FOCUS

____ Go over any homework assignments.

____ TWE, Teaching the Conversation, A–B, p. 208.

TEACH

____ TWE, *Después de conversar A*, p. 208.

____ TWE, Teaching Structure, *El futuro y el condicional*, A–C, p. 209.

____ TWE, *Práctica A–D*, pp. 209–210.

____ TWE, Teaching Structure, *Los complementos*, A–B, p. 210.

____ TWE, *Práctica E–F*, p. 211.

—*end of 45-minute lesson*

____ TWE, *Actividades comunicativas A–B*, p. 211.

—*end of 55-minute lesson*

ENRICHMENT / EXPANSION

____ CD-ROM, Disc 1, *Juegos de repaso*, Chapters 5–7.

CLOSE

____ WKBK, Self-Test 2, *Act. A–I*, pp. 82–86.

HOMEWORK ASSIGNMENTS	TEACHER NOTES

Teacher's Name _____ Date _____

Class(es) _____ Date(s) _____ M Tu W Th F

LOCAL OBJECTIVES	**BRR:** Bell Ringer Review **STM:** Student Tape Manual **TWE:** Teacher's Wraparound Edition **WKBK:** Workbook **CQ:** Chapter Quizzes
	Lesson Objectives: The students will review the vocabulary and structures from *Capitulos 5–7* and use them successfully in the *Repaso* activities.

FOCUS

_____ Correct WKBK, Self-Test 2, *Act. A–I*, pp. 82–86.

—*end of 45-minute lesson*

_____ Choose one or more Tasks from Performance Assessment, Tasks 5–7, to administer in addition to or instead of the Unit Test.

—*end of 55-minute lesson*

ASSESS

_____ Testing Program, Unit Test: Capítulos 5–7, pp. 53–56, p. 132; Speaking Test p. 176.

ENRICHMENT / EXPANSION

_____ TWE, **Learning From Photos**, p. 208.

_____ TWE, **Additional Practice**, p. 209.

_____ TWE, **Did You Know?** p. 209.

_____ TWE, **Learning From Photos**, p. 210.

_____ TWE, **Learning From Realia**, p. 210.

_____ TWE, **About the Spanish Language**, p. 211.

_____ TWE, **Learning From Photos**, p. 211.

CLOSE

_____ TWE, *Vistas de Costa Rica*, pp. 212–215.

HOMEWORK ASSIGNMENTS	TEACHER NOTES

Teacher's Name _____ Date _____

Class(es) _____ Date(s) _____ M Tu W Th F

LOCAL OBJECTIVES	**BRR:** Bell Ringer Review **STM:** Student Tape Manual **TWE:** Teacher's Wraparound Edition **WKBK:** Workbook **CQ:** Chapter Quizzes
	Chapter Objectives: The students will • talk about accidents and medical problems. • talk about hospital stays. • discuss things that they and others have done recently. • compare things with like characteristics. • talk about health care in various areas of the Spanish-speaking world.
	Note to teacher: For all Lesson Plan activities based on the student textbook you may use the CD-ROM version of ¡*Buen viaje!* The CD-ROM is also an excellent reinforcement tool for students to use on those days when the class does not meet. **FOCUS** ____ Go over any homework assignments. ____ Give an overview of the chapter and explain TWE, **Chapter Projects**, p. 217. ____ TWE, BRR, p. 218.
	TEACH ____ TWE, Teaching Vocabulary, *Palabras 1,* A–E, pp. 218–219. Use STM, *Actividad A* p. 82 (Cassette 5B/CD-5). ____ TWE, *Práctica A–D,* pp. 220–221. ____ TWE, *Actividad comunicativa A,* p. 221. *—end of 45-minute lesson* ____ TWE, **Pantomime 1–2**, p. 218. ____ TWE, **Learning From Photos**, p. 221. *—end of 55-minute lesson*
	ASSESS ____ TWE, Informal Assessment, p. 219.
	ENRICHMENT / EXPANSION ____ TWE, **Spotlight on Culture**, p. 217. ____ TWE, **About the Spanish Language**, p. 219. ____ TWE, Expansion, *Práctica B,* p. 220. ____ TWE, Writing Development, p. 220. ____ TWE, **Did You Know?**, p. 220.
	CLOSE ____ TWE, *Juego,* p. 221. ____ WKBK, *Act. A–C,* pp. 87–88.

Teacher's Name _____ Date _____

Class(es) _____ Date(s) _____ M Tu W Th F

LOCAL OBJECTIVES	
	BRR: Bell Ringer Review **STM:** Student Tape Manual **TWE:** Teacher's Wraparound Edition **WKBK:** Workbook **CQ:** Chapter Quizzes
	Chapter Objectives: The students will • talk about accidents and medical problems. • talk about hospital stays. • discuss things that they and others have done recently. • compare things with like characteristics. • talk about health care in various areas of the Spanish-speaking world.
	FOCUS ____ Go over any homework assignments. ____ TWE, BRR, p. 222.
	TEACH ____ TWE, Teaching Vocabulary, *Palabras 2*, A–C, pp. 222–223. Use STM, *Actividad* D, p. 85 (Cassette 5B/CD-5). ____ TWE, *Práctica A–D*, pp. 224–225. ____ TWE, **Learning From Photos**, p. 224. ____ TWE, *Actividades comunicativas A–B*, p. 225. *—end of 45-minute lesson* ____ TWE, **Vocabulary Expansion**, p. 223. ____ TWE, Expansion, p. 223. *—end of 55-minute lesson*
	ENRICHMENT / EXPANSION ____ TWE, **About the Spanish Language**, p. 222. ____ TWE, Expansion, *Práctica A–B*, p. 224. ____ TWE, **Learning From Realia**, p. 224. ____ TWE, **Learning From Photos**, p. 225.
	CLOSE ____ WKBK, *Act. D–E*, pp. 88–89.

	HOMEWORK ASSIGNMENTS	TEACHER NOTES

Teacher's Name _____ Date _____

Class(es) _____ Date(s) _____ M Tu W Th F

LOCAL OBJECTIVES	
BRR: Bell Ringer Review **TWE:** Teacher's Wraparound Edition **CQ:** Chapter Quizzes	**STM:** Student Tape Manual **WKBK:** Workbook

Chapter Objectives: The students will

- talk about accidents and medical problems.
- talk about hospital stays.
- discuss things that they and others have done recently.
- compare things with like characteristics.
- talk about health care in various areas of the Spanish-speaking world.

FOCUS

_____ Go over any homework assignments.

_____ Review vocabulary using Vocabulary Transparencies 8.1 (A&B).

TEACH

_____ STM, *Actividades B–C*, pp. 83–84, *E–F*, pp. 85–86 (Cassette 5B/CD-5).

_____ TWE, Teaching Structure, *El presente perfecto*, A–C, pp. 226–227.

_____ TWE, *Práctica A–C*, p. 227.

_____ STM, *Actividad A*, p. 87 (Cassette 5B/CD-5).

—end of 45-minute lesson

_____ Write a combination of 20–25 *-ar, -er, -ir* infinitives on the board. Call students to the board and have them write the past participle next to the infinitive.

_____ Write the forms of *haber* on the board. Make up questions using *haber* and the past participles already on the board. Call on students to respond, pointing to the words as necessary.

—end of 55-minute lesson

ASSESS

_____ CQ, Quizzes 1, 2, pp. 35–36.

ENRICHMENT / EXPANSION

_____ TWE, Writing Development, p. 227.

_____ TWE, **Learning From Realia**, p. 227.

CLOSE

_____ WKBK, *Act. A*, p. 89.

HOMEWORK ASSIGNMENTS	TEACHER NOTES

Teacher's Name _____ Date_____

Class(es) _____Date(s) _____ M Tu W Th F

LOCAL OBJECTIVES	**BRR:** Bell Ringer Review **TWE:** Teacher's Wraparound Edition **CQ:** Chapter Quizzes	**STM:** Student Tape Manual **WKBK:** Workbook

Chapter Objectives: The students will

- talk about accidents and medical problems.
- talk about hospital stays.
- discuss things that they and others have done recently.
- compare things with like characteristics.
- talk about health care in various areas of the Spanish-speaking world.

FOCUS

____ Go over any homework assignments.

____ TWE, BRR, p. 226.

TEACH

____ TWE, *Práctica D*, p. 228.

____ TWE, *Actividad comunicativa A*, p. 228.

____ TWE, Teaching Structure, *Los participios irregulares*, p. 228.

____ TWE, *Práctica A–B*, pp. 228–229.

____ TWE, *Actividades comunicativas A–B*, p. 229.

____ STM, *Actividad B*, p. 87–88 (Cassette 5B/CD-5).

—*end of 45-minute lesson*

____ Make up a variety of questions using the present perfect with irregular past participles. Call on students to answer orally.

____ TWE, Expansion, *Práctica D*, p. 228.

—*end of 55-minute lesson*

ENRICHMENT / EXPANSION

____ TWE, **Learning From Photos**, p. 229.

____ TWE, **Did You Know?**, p. 229.

CLOSE

____ WKBK, *Act. B–C*, p. 90.

HOMEWORK ASSIGNMENTS	TEACHER NOTES

Teacher's Name _____ Date _____

Class(es) _____ Date(s) _____ M Tu W Th F

LOCAL OBJECTIVES	
	BRR: Bell Ringer Review **STM:** Student Tape Manual **TWE:** Teacher's Wraparound Edition **WKBK:** Workbook **CQ:** Chapter Quizzes

Chapter Objectives: The students will

- talk about accidents and medical problems.
- talk about hospital stays.
- discuss things that they and others have done recently.
- compare things with like characteristics.
- talk about health care in various areas of the Spanish-speaking world.

FOCUS

____ Go over any homework assignments.

____ TWE, BRR, p. 228.

TEACH

____ TWE, Teaching Structure, *Comparación de igualdad*, A–B, p. 230.

____ TWE, *Práctica A–B*, pp. 230–231.

____ TWE, *Actividad comunicativa A*, p. 231.

____ STM, *Actividades C–D*, pp. 88–89 (Cassette 5B/CD-5).

—end of 45-minute lesson

____ Model some sample comparisons of students in class. (*Miguel es tan alto como Juan. María es tan amable como Estela.*) Now call on students to make comparisons among their classmates. (Remind students to be careful not to hurt anyone's feelings.)

____ Show Vocabulary Transparencies again. Call on pairs of students to come to the overhead. Give TPR commands. (*Toquen la pierna. Toquen la cara*).

—end of 55-minute lesson

ENRICHMENT / EXPANSION

____ TWE, Technology Option, p. 231.

____ TWE, **Learning From Realia**, p. 231.

____ Choose a variety of activities from the Expansion Activities Booklet.

CLOSE

____ WKBK, *Act. D–E*, p. 91.

HOMEWORK ASSIGNMENTS	TEACHER NOTES

Teacher's Name _____ Date _____

Class(es) _____ Date(s) _____ M Tu W Th F

LOCAL OBJECTIVES	**BRR:** Bell Ringer Review **STM:** Student Tape Manual **TWE:** Teacher's Wraparound Edition **WKBK:** Workbook **CQ:** Chapter Quizzes

Chapter Objectives: The students will

- talk about accidents and medical problems.
- talk about hospital stays.
- discuss things that they and others have done recently.
- compare things with like characteristics.
- talk about health care in various areas of the Spanish-speaking world.

FOCUS

_____ Go over any homework assignments.

_____ TWE, BRR, p. 230.

TEACH

_____ TWE, Teaching the Conversation, A–D, p. 232. Use STM, *Actividades E–F*, pp. 89–90 and Cassette 5B/CD-5.

_____ TWE, *Después de conversar*, p. 232.

_____ TWE, *Actividades comunicativas A–C*, p. 233.

_____ STM, *Actividades A–F*, pp. 90–95 (Cassette 5B/CD-5).

—*end of 45-minute lesson*

_____ Have students work in pairs to develop true comparative statements about classmates, teachers, or places in their city or state. Call on students to make their comparisons orally and have the class agree or disagree. If the students disagree, they tell why. After all the students have had a chance to participate, choose 10 comparative statements and take a poll. Make a graph from the answer and then have students interpret the graph.

_____ Have students complete the following paragraph with original sentences of their own. For example: *Voy a graduarme en mayo. Mis padres me han permitido tener una gran fiesta. Yo he reservado el salón de baile en el hotel Tejas. También ya he...* Turn in paragraph.

—*end of 55-minute lesson*

ASSESS

_____ CQ, Quizzes 3, 4, pp. 37–38.

ENRICHMENT / EXPANSION

_____ TWE, Technology Option, p. 232.

_____ TWE, Technology Option, p. 233.

_____ TWE, **Learning From Photos**, p. 233.

CLOSE

_____ TWE, **Cooperative Learning**, p. 233.

Teacher's Name _____ Date _____

Class(es) _____ Date(s) _____ M Tu W Th F

LOCAL OBJECTIVES	
	BRR: Bell Ringer Review **STM:** Student Tape Manual **TWE:** Teacher's Wraparound Edition **WKBK:** Workbook **CQ:** Chapter Quizzes

Chapter Objectives: The students will

- talk about accidents and medical problems.
- talk about hospital stays.
- discuss things that they and others have done recently.
- compare things with like characteristics.
- talk about health care in various areas of the Spanish-speaking world.

FOCUS

____ Go over any homework assignments.

____ Have students write as much as they can in five minutes about Communication Transparency C–8.

TEACH

____ TWE, Teaching the Reading, *Practicantes*, p. 234.

____ TWE, *Después de leer*, A–C, p. 235.

____ TWE, *Tecnotur*, Video A–B, p. 243.

____ TWE, *Actividades comunicativas A–C*, p. 240.

____ TWE, *Actividades escritas A–B*, p. 241.

—end of 45-minute lesson

____ TWE, **Learning From Photos**, p. 234.

____ TWE, **Learning From Realia**, p. 235.

—end of 55-minute lesson

ASSESS

____ CQ, Quiz 5, p. 39.

ENRICHMENT / EXPANSION

____ TWE, *Lectura opcional 1*, p. 236.

____ TWE, **Did You Know?**, p. 236.

____ TWE, *Lectura opcional 2*, p. 237.

____ TWE, **Learning from Realia**, p. 237.

____ TWE, **About the Spanish Language**, p. 237.

____ TWE, **Career Connection**, p. 240.

____ TWE, **History Connection**, p. 240.

____ TWE, **Critical Thinking Activity**, p. 240.

____ TWE, Technology Option, p. 241.

CLOSE

____ TWE, Writing Strategy, A–B, p. 241.

Teacher's Name _____ Date _____

Class(es) _____ Date(s) _____ M Tu W Th F

LOCAL OBJECTIVES	**BRR:** Bell Ringer Review **TWE:** Teacher's Wraparound Edition **CQ:** Chapter Quizzes	**STM:** Student Tape Manual **WKBK:** Workbook

Chapter Objectives: The students will

- talk about accidents and medical problems.
- talk about hospital stays.
- discuss things that they and others have done recently.
- compare things with like characteristics.
- talk about health care in various areas of the Spanish-speaking world.

FOCUS

_____ Go over any homework assignments.

_____ Show Communication Transparency C–8 and have the students describe it.

—*end of 45-minute lesson*

_____ Use Situation Cards to review *Capítulo 8*.

—*end of 55-minute lesson*

ASSESS

_____ Testing Program, *Capítulo 8*, pp. 57–62, p. 133; Speaking Test p. 177, Proficiency Test p. 197.

ENRICHMENT / EXPANSION

_____ TWE, *Conexiones, Las ciencias*, pp. 238–239.

_____ TWE, **Learning From Photos**, p. 238.

_____ TWE, **Learning From Realia**, p. 239.

_____ WKBK, *Act. A–C*, pp. 94.

CLOSE

_____ WKBK, *Mi autobiografía*, p. 94.

HOMEWORK ASSIGNMENTS	TEACHER NOTES

Teacher's Name _____ Date _____

Class(es) _____ Date(s) _____ M Tu W Th F

LOCAL OBJECTIVES	**BRR:** Bell Ringer Review **STM:** Student Tape Manual
	TWE: Teacher's Wraparound Edition **WKBK:** Workbook
	CQ: Chapter Quizzes

Chapter Objectives: The students will

- talk about life in the city.
- talk about life in the country.
- describe things that were happening.
- refer to things already mentioned.
- indicate where things are located.
- talk about some cities in the Spanish-speaking world.

Note to teacher: For all Lesson Plan activities based on the student textbook you may use the CD-ROM version of ¡*Buen viaje!* The CD-ROM is also an excellent reinforcement tool for students to use on those days when the class does not meet.

FOCUS

_____ Go over any homework assignments.

_____ Give an overview of the chapter and explain TWE, **Chapter Projects**, p. 245.

_____ TWE, BRR, p. 246.

TEACH

_____ TWE, Teaching Vocabulary, *Palabras 1,* A–D, pp. 246-247. Use STM, *Actividad A,* pp. 96–97 (Cassette 6A/CD-5).

_____ TWE, **Pantomime**, p. 246.

_____ TWE, *Práctica A–D,* pp. 248–249.

_____ TWE, *Actividades comunicativas A–B,* p. 249.

—end of 45-minute lesson

_____ TWE, **Additional Practice**, p. 247.

_____ TWE, Expansion, *Práctica A,* p. 248.

_____ TWE, Writing Development, p. 248.

—end of 55-minute lesson

ENRICHMENT / EXPANSION

_____ TWE, **Spotlight on Culture**, p. 245.

_____ TWE, **Learning From Photos**, p. 247.

_____ TWE, **About the Spanish Language,** p. 247.

_____ TWE, Writing Development, p. 249.

_____ TWE, **Learning From Photos**, p. 249.

CLOSE

_____ WKBK, *Act. A–C,* pp. 95–96.

Teacher's Name _____ Date _____

Class(es) _____ Date(s) _____ M Tu W Th F

LOCAL OBJECTIVES	**BRR:** Bell Ringer Review **TWE:** Teacher's Wraparound Edition **CQ:** Chapter Quizzes	**STM:** Student Tape Manual **WKBK:** Workbook

Chapter Objectives: The students will

- talk about life in the city.
- talk about life in the country.
- describe things that were happening.
- refer to things already mentioned.
- indicate where things are located.
- talk about some cities in the Spanish-speaking world.

FOCUS

_____ Go over any homework.

_____ TWE, BRR, p. 250.

TEACH

_____ TWE, Teaching Vocabulary, *Palabras* 2, A–C, p. 250. Use STM, *Actividad* D, p. 98 (Cassette 6A/CD-5).

_____ TWE, *Práctica A–C*, pp. 252–253.

_____ TWE, *Actividades comunicativas A–B*, p. 253.

_____ TWE, **Learning From Photos**, p. 251.

—*end of 45-minute lesson*

_____ TWE, Expansion, *Práctica A*, p. 252.

_____ TWE, Technology Option, p. 253.

—*end of 55-minute lesson*

ENRICHMENT / EXPANSION

_____ TWE, **Vocabulary Expansion**, p. 250.

_____ TWE, **Vocabulary Expansion**, p. 251.

_____ TWE, **Learning from Photos**, p. 252.

_____ TWE, **Learning from Photos**, p. 253.

CLOSE

_____ TWE, **Pantomime**, p. 250.

_____ WKBK, *Act. D–F,* pp. 97–98.

HOMEWORK ASSIGNMENTS	TEACHER NOTES

Teacher's Name _____ Date _____

Class(es) _____ Date(s) _____ M Tu W Th F

LOCAL OBJECTIVES	**BRR:** Bell Ringer Review **TWE:** Teacher's Wraparound Edition **CQ:** Chapter Quizzes	**STM:** Student Tape Manual **WKBK:** Workbook

Chapter Objectives: The students will

- talk about life in the city.
- talk about life in the country.
- describe things that were happening.
- refer to things already mentioned.
- indicate where things are located.
- talk about some cities in the Spanish-speaking world.

FOCUS

_____ Go over any homework.

_____ Review all vocabulary using Vocabulary Transparencies 9.1 (A&B) and 9.2 (A&B).

TEACH

_____ STM, *Actividades B–C*, pp. 97–98, *E–F*, pp. 99–100. (Cassette 6A/ CD-5).

_____ TWE, Teaching Structure, *El imperfecto progresivo*, A–C, p. 254.

_____ TWE, *Práctica A–C*, pp. 254–255.

—end of 45-minute lesson

_____ Call students to the overhead projector to do TPR activities, using Vocabulary Transparencies 8.1 (A&B). (*Toquen la guagua. Señalen la plaza.*)

_____ Follow up with single true/false statements. Point to a picture. (*Es una boca del metro.*)

—end of 55-minute lesson

ASSESS

_____ CQ, Quizzes 1, 2, pp. 40–41.

ENRICHMENT / EXPANSION

_____ TWE, Writing Development, p. 255.

_____ TWE, Expansion, *Actividad comunicativa* B, p. 255.

CLOSE

_____ WKBK, *Act. A–B*, p. 99.

HOMEWORK ASSIGNMENTS	**TEACHER NOTES**

Teacher's Name _____Date_____

Class(es) _____Date(s) _____ M Tu W Th F

LOCAL OBJECTIVES	**BRR:** Bell Ringer Review **TWE:** Teacher's Wraparound Edition **CQ:** Chapter Quizzes	**STM:** Student Tape Manual **WKBK:** Workbook

Chapter Objectives: The students will

- talk about life in the city.
- talk about life in the country.
- describe things that were happening.
- refer to things already mentioned.
- indicate where things are located.
- talk about some cities in the Spanish-speaking world.

FOCUS

_____ Go over any homework assignments.

_____ TWE, BRR, p. 254.

TEACH

_____ TWE, *Actividades comunicativas A–B*, p. 255.

_____ STM, *Actividades A–B*, pp. 100–101 (Cassette 6A/CD-5).

_____ TWE, Teaching Structure, *Colocación de los pronombres de complemento*, A–B, p. 256.

_____ TWE, *Práctica A–E*, pp. 256–257.

—end of 45-minute lesson

_____ STM, *Actividades C–D*, pp. 100–101 (Cassette 6A/CD-5).

—end of 55-minute lesson

CLOSE

_____ WKBK, *Act. C–E*, pp. 100–101.

_____ TWE, *Tecnotur*, Video A–B, p. 313.

	HOMEWORK ASSIGNMENTS	TEACHER NOTES

Teacher's Name _____ Date_____

Class(es) _____ Date(s) _____ M Tu W Th F

LOCAL OBJECTIVES	**BRR:** Bell Ringer Review **STM:** Student Tape Manual
	TWE: Teacher's Wraparound Edition **WKBK:** Workbook
	CQ: Chapter Quizzes

Chapter Objectives: The students will

- talk about life in the city.
- talk about life in the country.
- describe things that were happening.
- refer to things already mentioned.
- indicate where things are located.
- talk about some cities in the Spanish-speaking world.

FOCUS

_____ Go over any homework assignments.

_____ TWE, BRR, p. 258.

TEACH

_____ TWE, Teaching Structure, *Adjetivos y pronombres demostrativos*, A–D, p. 258.

_____ TWE, *Práctica A–B*, p. 259.

_____ TWE, *Actividad comunicativa A*, p. 259.

_____ STM, *Actividad E*, p. 102 (Cassette 6A/CD-5).

—*end of 45-minute lesson*

_____ TWE, *Juego*, p. 259.

—*end of 55-minute lesson*

ENRICHMENT / EXPANSION

_____ TWE, **About the Spanish Language**, p. 258.

_____ TWE, **Learning From Realia**, p.259.

CLOSE

_____ Choose a variety of activities from the Expansion Activities Booklet.

_____ WKBK, *Act. F–G*, p. 102.

HOMEWORK ASSIGNMENTS	TEACHER NOTES

Teacher's Name _____ Date _____

Class(es) _____ Date(s) _____ M Tu W Th F

LOCAL OBJECTIVES	**BRR:** Bell Ringer Review **TWE:** Teacher's Wraparound Edition **CQ:** Chapter Quizzes	**STM:** Student Tape Manual **WKBK:** Workbook
	Chapter Objectives: The students will • talk about life in the city. • talk about life in the country. • describe things that were happening. • refer to things already mentioned. • indicate where things are located. • talk about some cities in the Spanish-speaking world.	
	FOCUS ____ Go over any homework assignments. ____ TWE, BRR, p. 260.	
	TEACH ____ TWE, Teaching the Conversation, A–E, p. 260. Use STM, *Actividades F–G*, p. 103 (Cassette 6A/CD-5). ____ TWE, *Después de conversar*, p. 260. ____ TWE, *Actividades comunicativas A–B*, p. 261. ____ STM, *Actividades A–C*, pp. 104–107 (Cassette 6A/CD-5). —*end of 45-minute lesson* ____ TWE, Technology Option, p. 260. ____ TWE, **Learning From Photos**, p. 261. —*end of 55-minute lesson*	
	ASSESS ____ CQ, Quizzes 3–5, pp. 42–44.	
	ENRICHMENT / EXPANSION ____ TWE, Technology Option, p. 261. ____ WKBK, *Act. A–E*, pp. 103–105.	
	CLOSE ____ TWE, Pre-reading activity, p. 262.	
	HOMEWORK ASSIGNMENTS	**TEACHER NOTES**

Teacher's Name _____ Date _____

Class(es) _____ Date(s) _____ M Tu W Th F

LOCAL OBJECTIVES	
	BRR: Bell Ringer Review **STM:** Student Tape Manual **TWE:** Teacher's Wraparound Edition **WKBK:** Workbook **CQ:** Chapter Quizzes

Chapter Objectives: The students will

- talk about life in the city.
- talk about life in the country.
- describe things that were happening.
- refer to things already mentioned.
- indicate where things are located.
- talk about some cities in the Spanish-speaking world.

FOCUS

_____ Go over any homework assignments.

_____ TWE, BRR, p. 262.

TEACH

_____ TWE, *Tecnotur,* Video, A–B, p. 271.

_____ TWE, Teaching the Reading, *Buenos Aires, Argentina,* pp. 262–263.

_____ TWE, *Después de leer A,* p. 263.

_____ TWE, *Actividades orales A–C,* p. 268.

_____ TWE, *Actividad escrita A,* p. 269.

—*end of 45-minute lesson*

_____ TWE, Technology Option, p. 263.

_____ TWE, *Juego,* p. 268.

—*end of 55-minute lesson*

ENRICHMENT / EXPANSION

_____ TWE, **About the Spanish Language**, p. 262.

_____ TWE, *Lectura opcional 1,* p. 264.

_____ TWE, **Did You Know?**, p. 264.

_____ TWE, *Lectura opcional 2,* p. 265.

_____ TWE, **Learning From Photos**, p. 265.

_____ TWE, Technology Option, p. 268.

_____ TWE, **Learning From Photos**, p. 268.

_____ TWE, **Learning From Photos**, p. 269.

CLOSE

_____ WKBK, *Mi autobiografía,* p. 106.

Teacher's Name _____ Date _____

Class(es) _____ Date(s) _____ M Tu W Th F

LOCAL OBJECTIVES	
	BRR: Bell Ringer Review **STM:** Student Tape Manual **TWE:** Teacher's Wraparound Edition **WKBK:** Workbook **CQ:** Chapter Quizzes

Chapter Objectives: The students will

- talk about life in the city.
- talk about life in the country.
- describe things that were happening.
- refer to things already mentioned.
- indicate where things are located.
- talk about some cities in the Spanish-speaking world.

FOCUS

____ Go over any homework assignments.

____ Use Situation Cards, *Capítulo 9,* to review.

—*end of 45-minute lesson*

____ Review using Vocabulary Transparencies 9.1 (A&B) and 9.2 (A&B).

____ Show Communication Transparency C–9 for review.

—*end of 55-minute lesson*

ASSESS

____ Testing Program, *Capítulo 9,* pp. 63–67, p. 134; Speaking Test p. 178, Proficiency Test p. 198.

ENRICHMENT / EXPANSION

____ TWE, *Conexiones, Las ciencias sociales,* pp. 266–267.

____ TWE, **Learning From Photos**, p. 266.

CLOSE

____ TWE, Writing Strategy, A–B, p. 269.

HOMEWORK ASSIGNMENTS	TEACHER NOTES

Teacher's Name _____ Date _____

Class(es) _____ Date(s) _____ M Tu W Th F

LOCAL OBJECTIVES	**BRR:** Bell Ringer Review **TWE:** Teacher's Wraparound Edition **CQ:** Chapter Quizzes	**STM:** Student Tape Manual **WKBK:** Workbook

Chapter Objectives: The students will

- talk about foods and food preparation.
- give commands.
- refer to people and things previously mentioned.
- prepare some regional specialties.
- talk about the origin of several foods.

Note to teacher: For all Lesson Plan activities based on the student textbook you may use the CD-ROM version of *¡Buen viaje!* The CD-ROM is also an excellent reinforcement tool for students to use on those days when the class does not meet.

FOCUS

____ Go over any homework.

____ Give an overview of the chapter and explain TWE, **Chapter Projects**, p. 273.

____ TWE, BRR, p. 274.

TEACH

____ TWE, Teaching Vocabulary, *Palabras 1,* A–C, p. 274. Show Vocabulary Transparencies 10.1 (A&B) and introduce and practice the new words. You may also wish to use STM *Actividad A,* p. 108 (Cassette 6B/CD-6).

____ TWE, *Práctica A–D,* pp. 276–277.

____ TWE, Expansion, *Práctica A,* p. 276.

____ TWE, *Actividades comunicativas A–B,* p. 277.

—end of 45-minute lesson

____ TWE, **Pantomime**, p. 274.

____ TWE, **Cooperative Learning**, p. 275.

—end of 55-minute lesson

ENRICHMENT / EXPANSION

____ TWE, **Spotlight on Culture**, p. 273.

CLOSE

____ WKBK, *Act. A–D,* pp. 107–108.

	HOMEWORK ASSIGNMENTS	TEACHER NOTES

Teacher's Name _____ Date _____

Class(es) _____ Date(s) _____ M Tu W Th F

LOCAL OBJECTIVES	**BRR:** Bell Ringer Review **STM:** Student Tape Manual **TWE:** Teacher's Wraparound Edition **WKBK:** Workbook **CQ:** Chapter Quizzes

Chapter Objectives: The students will

- talk about foods and food preparation.
- give commands.
- refer to people and things previously mentioned.
- prepare some regional specialties.
- talk about the origin of several foods.

FOCUS

____ Go over any homework assignments.

____ TWE, BRR, p. 278.

TEACH

____ TWE, Teaching Vocabulary, *Palabras 2*, A–C, p. 278. Show Vocabulary Transparencies 10.2 (A&B) and introduce and practice the new words. You may also wish to use STM *Actividad D*, p. 111 (Cassette 6B/CD-6).

____ TWE, **Pantomime**, p. 278.

____ TWE, *Práctica A–D*, pp. 280–281.

____ TWE, *Actividad comunicativa A*, p. 281.

—*end of 45-minute lesson*

____ TWE, *Juego*, p. 281.

—*end of 55-minute lesson*

ENRICHMENT / EXPANSION

____ TWE, **About the Spanish Language**, p. 279.

____ TWE, **Learning From Realia**, p. 281.

CLOSE

____ WKBK, *Act. E–I*, pp. 109–111.

HOMEWORK ASSIGNMENTS	TEACHER NOTES

Teacher's Name _____ Date _____

Class(es) _____ Date(s) _____ M Tu W Th F

LOCAL OBJECTIVES	**BRR:** Bell Ringer Review **STM:** Student Tape Manual
	TWE: Teacher's Wraparound Edition **WKBK:** Workbook **CQ:** Chapter Quizzes

Chapter Objectives: The students will

- talk about foods and food preparation.
- give commands.
- refer to people and things previously mentioned.
- prepare some regional specialties.
- talk about the origin of several foods.

FOCUS

____ Go over any homework assignments.

____ TWE, **Learning From Photos**, p. 277.

TEACH

____ STM, *Actividades B–C*, pp. 109–110, *E–F*, pp. 112 (Cassette 6B/CD-6).

____ Ask the students questions using the vocabulary. (*¿Te gusta el pepino en la ensalada? ¿Te gusta el té con limón?*)

____ Students work in pairs to write about food and beverages that are consumed in the U.S. (*Se comen muchas hamburguesas.*)

____ TWE, Teaching Structure, *Imperativo formal: formas regulares*, A–C, p. 282.

____ TWE, *Práctica A–B*, p. 283.

—*end of 45-minute lesson*

____ Write the following categories on the board horizontally: *Verduras, Frutas, Verbos, Utensilios/Electrodomésticos*. Call on students to go to the board. Give two vocabulary words from *Palabras 1* or *Palabras 2*. The students write them under the correct category.

—*end of 55-minute lesson*

ASSESS

____ CQ, Quizzes 1, 2, pp. 45–46.

ENRICHMENT / EXPANSION

____ TWE, **Learning From Photos**, p. 282.

____ TWE, **Learning From Photos**, p. 283.

CLOSE

____ WKBK, *Act. A–B*, p. 112.

HOMEWORK ASSIGNMENTS	TEACHER NOTES

Teacher's Name _____ Date _____

Class(es) _____ Date(s) _____ M Tu W Th F

LOCAL OBJECTIVES	**BRR:** Bell Ringer Review **TWE:** Teacher's Wraparound Edition **CQ:** Chapter Quizzes	**STM:** Student Tape Manual **WKBK:** Workbook

	Chapter Objectives: The students will • talk about foods and food preparation. • give commands. • refer to people and things previously mentioned. • prepare some regional specialties. • talk about the origin of several foods.

	FOCUS ____ Go over any homework assignments. ____ TWE, BRR, p. 282.

	TEACH ____ TWE, *Práctica C-D,* p. 284. ____ TWE, Teaching Structure, *Imperativo formal: formas irregulares,* A–B, p. 285. ____ TWE, *Práctica A–C,* pp. 285–286. ____ TWE, *Actividad comunicativa A,* p. 286. ____ STM, *Actividades A–C,* pp. 113–114 (Cassette 6B/CD-6). *—end of 45-minute lesson* ____ TWE, *Actividad comunicativa A,* p. 284. ____ Have students write 3–5 commands that you normally tell them to do. (*No hablen. Cierren los libros.*) ____ Have students share their commands orally with the class. *—end of 55-minute lesson*

	ENRICHMENT / EXPANSION ____ TWE, **Fine Art Connection,** p. 284. ____ TWE, Expansion, *Práctica C,* p. 286.

	CLOSE ____ TWE, *Juego,* p. 286. ____ WKBK, *Act. C–D,* p. 113.

	HOMEWORK ASSIGNMENTS	**TEACHER NOTES**

Teacher's Name _____ Date _____

Class(es) _____ Date(s) _____ M Tu W Th F

LOCAL OBJECTIVES	
	BRR: Bell Ringer Review **STM:** Student Tape Manual **TWE:** Teacher's Wraparound Edition **WKBK:** Workbook **CQ:** Chapter Quizzes

Chapter Objectives: The students will

- talk about foods and food preparation.
- give commands.
- refer to people and things previously mentioned.
- prepare some regional specialties.
- talk about the origin of several foods.

FOCUS

____ Go over any homework assignments.

____ TWE, BRR, p. 287.

TEACH

____ TWE, Teaching Structure, *Colocación de los pronombres de complemento*, A–B, p. 287.

____ TWE, *Práctica A–B*, p. 287.

____ STM, *Actividades D–E*, p. 115 (Cassette 6B/CD-6).

____ TWE, *Tecnotur*, Video A–B, p. 299.

—end of 45-minute lesson

____ Write 10–20 commands on the left-hand side of the board. Call on volunteers to use the command in a complete statement. (*Escriban.* —*Escriban sus nombres en el cuaderno.*)

—end of 55-minute lesson

ASSESS

____ CQ, Quizzes 3–4, pp. 47–48.

ENRICHMENT / EXPANSION

____ TWE, *Lectura opcional 1*, p. 292.

____ TWE, **About the Spanish Language**, p. 292.

____ TWE, *Lectura opcional 2*, p. 293.

____ TWE, **Did You Know?**, p. 293.

CLOSE

____ WKBK, *Act. E–F*, p. 114.

HOMEWORK ASSIGNMENTS	TEACHER NOTES

Teacher's Name _____ Date _____

Class(es) _____ Date(s) _____ M Tu W Th F

LOCAL OBJECTIVES	**BRR:** Bell Ringer Review	**STM:** Student Tape Manual
	TWE: Teacher's Wraparound Edition	**WKBK:** Workbook
	CQ: Chapter Quizzes	

Chapter Objectives: The students will

- talk about foods and food preparation.
- give commands.
- refer to people and things previously mentioned.
- prepare some regional specialties.
- talk about the origin of several foods.

FOCUS

____ Go over any homework assignments.

____ TWE, BRR, p. 288.

TEACH

____ TWE, Teaching the Conversation, A–D, p. 288. Use STM, *Actividades F–G*, p. 116 (Cassette 6B/CD-6).

____ TWE, *Después de conversar*, p. 288.

____ TWE, *Actividades comunicativas A–C*, p. 289.

____ STM, *Actividades A–D*, pp. 117–120 (Cassette 6B/CD-6).

—*end of 45-minute lesson*

____ TWE, **Learning From Photos**, p. 289.

____ TWE, Technology Option, p. 288.

—*end of 55-minute lesson*

ENRICHMENT / EXPANSION

____ TWE, Technology Option, p. 289.

____ WKBK, *Act. A–E*, pp. 115–117.

____ To prepare for tomorrow's reading assignment, have students collect their favorite Hispanic recipes to discuss or prepare for a class fiesta.

CLOSE

____ Working in small groups, have students give advice and suggestions to each other as to what they have to do to pass the course, get permission to go to a friend's birthday party, or what they will have to do to become a doctor. For example, students may say: *Para pasar la clase, estudien mucho. Entreguen su tarea. Traigan su libro a la clase.*

HOMEWORK ASSIGNMENTS	TEACHER NOTES

Teacher's Name _____ Date _____

Class(es) _____ Date(s) _____ M Tu W Th F

LOCAL OBJECTIVES	**BRR:** Bell Ringer Review **STM:** Student Tape Manual
	TWE: Teacher's Wraparound Edition **WKBK:** Workbook
	CQ: Chapter Quizzes

Chapter Objectives: The students will

- talk about food and food preparation.
- give commands.
- refer to people and things previously mentioned.
- prepare some regional specialties.
- talk about the origin of several foods.

FOCUS

____ Go over any homework assignments.

____ TWE, BRR, p. 290.

TEACH

____ TWE, Teaching the Reading, *Una receta española*, p. 290.

____ TWE, *Después de leer A–D*, p. 291.

____ TWE, *Actividades orales A–D*, p. 296.

____ TWE, *Actividad escrita A*, p. 297.

—*end of 45-minute lesson*

____ Choose a variety of activities from the Expansion Activities Booklet.

—*end of 55-minute lesson*

ASSESS

____ CQ, Quiz 5, p. 49.

ENRICHMENT / EXPANSION

____ TWE, **Did You Know?**, p. 290.

____ TWE, Technology Option, p. 291.

____ TWE, **Did You Know?**, p. 291.

____ TWE, **Critical Thinking Activity**, p. 291.

____ TWE, Technology Option, p. 296.

____ TWE, Technology Option, p. 297.

CLOSE

____ WKBK, *Mi autobiografía*, p. 118.

HOMEWORK ASSIGNMENTS	TEACHER NOTES

Teacher's Name _____ Date _____

Class(es) _____ Date(s) _____ M Tu W Th F

LOCAL OBJECTIVES	**BRR:** Bell Ringer Review **STM:** Student Tape Manual **TWE:** Teacher's Wraparound Edition **WKBK:** Workbook **CQ:** Chapter Quizzes

Chapter Objectives: The students will

- talk about food and food preparation.
- give commands.
- refer to people and things previously mentioned.
- prepare some regional specialties.
- talk about the origin of several foods.

FOCUS

_____ Use Vocabulary Transparencies 10.1 (A&B) and 10.2 (A&B) to review. Have students say as much as possible about the activities.

_____ Show Communication Transparency C–10 and discuss with the students.

_____ Review Chapter Objectives, TWE, p. 272, asking students to give examples of what they have learned.

—*end of 45-minute lesson*

_____ Use Situation Cards, *Capítulo 10*, to practice.

—*end of 55-minute lesson*

ASSESS

_____ Testing Program, *Capítulo 10*, pp. 68–73, p. 135, Speaking Test p. 179; Proficiency Test p. 199.

ENRICHMENT / EXPANSION

_____ TWE, *Conexiones, Las ciencias*, pp. 294–295.

_____ TWE, **Learning From Photos**, p. 294.

_____ TWE, **Learning From Photos**, p. 298.

_____ TWE, Internet, p. 299.

CLOSE

_____ TWE, Writing Strategy A–B, p. 297.

HOMEWORK ASSIGNMENTS	TEACHER NOTES

Teacher's Name _____ Date _____

Class(es) _____ Date(s) _____ M Tu W Th F

LOCAL OBJECTIVES	**BRR:** Bell Ringer Review **STM:** Student Tape Manual **TWE:** Teacher's Wraparound Edition **WKBK:** Workbook **CQ:** Chapter Quizzes

Chapter Objectives: The students will

- talk about cars and driving.
- give directions on the road.
- tell family and friends what to do and what not to do.
- talk about highways in the Hispanic world.

Note to teacher: For all Lesson Plan activities based on the student textbook you may use the CD-ROM version of ¡*Buen viaje!* The CD-ROM is also an excellent reinforcement tool for students to use on those days when the class does not meet.

FOCUS

_____ Go over any homework assignments.

_____ Give an overview of the chapter and explain TWE, **Chapter Projects**, p. 301.

_____ TWE, BRR, p. 302.

TEACH

_____ TWE, Teaching Vocabulary, *Palabras 1,* A–E, pp. 302–303.

_____ Use Vocabulary Transparencies 11.1 (A–B) and STM, *Actividad A,* p. 121 (Cassette 7A/CD-6) to practice the new vocabulary.

_____ TWE, **Pantomime**, p. 302.

_____ TWE, *Práctica A–D,* pp. 304–305.

_____ TWE, *Actividades comunicativas A–C,* p. 305.

—end of 45-minute lesson

_____ TWE, **Vocabulary Expansion**, p. 303.

_____ TWE, **Additional Practice**, p. 303.

—end of 55-minute lesson

ENRICHMENT / EXPANSION

_____ TWE, **Spotlight on Culture**, p. 301.

_____ TWE, **Did You Know?**, p. 303.

_____ TWE, Expansion, *Práctica C,* p. 304.

_____ TWE, Technology Option, p. 305.

CLOSE

_____ TWE, **Learning From Photos**, p. 305.

_____ WKBK, *Act. A–C,* pp. 119–120.

Teacher's Name _____ Date _____

Class(es) _____ Date(s) _____ M Tu W Th F

LOCAL OBJECTIVES	**BRR:** Bell Ringer Review **STM:** Student Tape Manual **TWE:** Teacher's Wraparound Edition **WKBK:** Workbook **CQ:** Chapter Quizzes

Chapter Objectives: The students will

- talk about cars and driving.
- give directions on the road.
- tell family and friends what to do and what not to do.
- talk about highways in the Hispanic world.

FOCUS

____ Go over any homework assignments.

____ Review yesterday's lesson using TPR activities with TWE, *Palabras 1*, pp. 302–303.

____ TWE, BRR, p. 306.

TEACH

____ TWE, Teaching Vocabulary, *Palabras 2*, A–B, p. 306. Use STM, *Actividad D*, p. 123 (Cassette 7A/CD-6).

____ TWE, *Práctica A–C*, pp. 308–309.

____ TWE, *Actividad comunicativa A–B*, p. 309.

—end of 45-minute lesson

____ TWE, **Vocabulary Expansion**, p. 307.

____ TWE, **Learning From Photos**, p. 308.

—end of 55-minute lesson

ENRICHMENT / EXPANSION

____ TWE, **About the Spanish Language**, p. 307.

____ TWE, Expansion, *Práctica A*, p. 308.

____ TWE, Writing Development, p. 309.

____ TWE, **Geography Connection**, p. 309.

CLOSE

____ WKBK, *Act. D–F*, pp. 121–122.

HOMEWORK ASSIGNMENTS	TEACHER NOTES

¡Buen viaje! LEVEL 2 LESSON PLAN CHAPTER 11: DAY 3

Teacher's Name _____ Date _____

Class(es) _____ Date(s) _____ M Tu W Th F

LOCAL OBJECTIVES	**BRR:** Bell Ringer Review **STM:** Student Tape Manual **TWE:** Teacher's Wraparound Edition **WKBK:** Workbook **CQ:** Chapter Quizzes
	Chapter Objectives: The students will • talk about cars and driving. • give directions on the road. • tell family and friends what to do and what not to do. • talk about highways in the Hispanic world.
	FOCUS _____ Go over any homework assignments. _____ Review vocabulary using Vocabulary Transparencies 11.1 and 11.2 (A&B).
	TEACH _____ STM, *Actividades B–C*, pp. 122–123, *E–F*, pp. 124–125 (Cassette 7A/CD-6). _____ TWE, Teaching Structure, *Imperativo familiar: formas regulares*, A–B, p. 310. _____ TWE, *Práctica* A–C, pp. 310–311. *—end of 45-minute lesson* _____ Paired Activity. Have students imagine that they have a younger brother/sister who is a toddler. Have them write 7–10 negative commands that they would say to their brother/sister so they won't get into trouble or get hurt. (*No corras. No te caigas en las escaleras. No comas tierra.*) Have students write commands on the board to generate one list. *—end of 55-minute lesson*
	ASSESS _____ CQ, Quizzes 1, 2, pp. 50–51.
	ENRICHMENT / EXPANSION _____ TWE, **Did You Know?**, p. 311. _____ TWE, **Learning From Realia**, p. 311.
	CLOSE _____ WKBK, *Act. A–B*, p. 123.
	HOMEWORK ASSIGNMENTS **TEACHER NOTES**

Teacher's Name _____ Date _____

Class(es) _____ Date(s) _____ M Tu W Th F

LOCAL OBJECTIVES	**BRR:** Bell Ringer Review **STM:** Student Tape Manual **TWE:** Teacher's Wraparound Edition **WKBK:** Workbook **CQ:** Chapter Quizzes

Chapter Objectives: The students will

- talk about cars and driving.
- give directions on the road.
- tell family and friends what to do and what not to do.
- talk about highways in the Hispanic world.

FOCUS

____ Go over any homework assignments.

____ TWE, BRR, p. 310.

TEACH

____ TWE, Teaching Structure, *Imperativo familiar: formas irregulares*, p. 312.

____ TWE, *Práctica A–C*, pp. 312–313.

____ TWE, *Actividades comunicativas A–B*, p. 313.

____ STM, *Actividades A–B*, pp. 125–126 (Cassette 7A/CD-6).

—*end of 45-minute lesson*

____ Make up commands and have students perform them. (*Habla con Juan. Cierra el libro.*)

____ Write all eight irregular commands on the board in a vertical sequence. Call on students to write a command using the verb of his/her choice. Continue until all students have had a chance to write. (Students cannot repeat the exact same command.)

—*end of 55-minute lesson*

ENRICHMENT / EXPANSION

____ TWE, **Did You Know?**, p. 312.

CLOSE

____ TWE, *Actividad comunicativa C*, p. 313.

____ WKBK, *Act. C–D*, p. 124.

HOMEWORK ASSIGNMENTS	TEACHER NOTES

Teacher's Name _____ Date _____

Class(es) _____ Date(s) _____ M Tu W Th F

LOCAL OBJECTIVES	**BRR:** Bell Ringer Review **TWE:** Teacher's Wraparound Edition **CQ:** Chapter Quizzes	**STM:** Student Tape Manual **WKBK:** Workbook

	Chapter Objectives: The students will • talk about cars and driving. • give directions on the road. • tell family and friends what to do and what not to do. • talk about highways in the Hispanic world.

	FOCUS _____ Go over any homework assignments. _____ TWE, BRR, p. 314.

	TEACH _____ TWE, Teaching Structure, *Imperativo negativo*, A–B, p. 314. _____ TWE, *Práctica A–E*, pp. 314–315. _____ STM, *Actividad C*, p. 126 (Cassette 7A/CD-6). _____ TWE, Teaching the Conversation, A–D, p. 316. Use STM, *Actividades D–E*, p. 127 (Cassette 7A/CD-6). _____ TWE, *Después de conversar*, p. 316. *—end of 45-minute lesson* _____ TWE, Expansion, *Práctica B*, p. 315. _____ TWE, **Learning From Photos**, p. 315. *—end of 55-minute lesson*

	ENRICHMENT / EXPANSION _____ TWE, Technology Option, p. 316. _____ TWE, **About the Spanish Language**, p. 316. _____ TWE, **History Connection**, p. 317.

	CLOSE _____ TWE, *Juego*, p. 317. _____ WKBK, *Act. E–G*, pp. 125–126.

	HOMEWORK ASSIGNMENTS	**TEACHER NOTES**

Teacher's Name _____ Date _____

Class(es) _____ Date(s) _____ M Tu W Th F

LOCAL OBJECTIVES	**BRR:** Bell Ringer Review **TWE:** Teacher's Wraparound Edition **CQ:** Chapter Quizzes	**STM:** Student Tape Manual **WKBK:** Workbook

Chapter Objectives: The students will

- talk about cars and driving.
- give directions on the road.
- tell family and friends what to do and what not to do.
- talk about highways in the Hispanic world.

FOCUS

____ Go over any homework assignments.

____ TWE, *Actividad comunicativa A*, p. 317.

TEACH

____ STM, *Actividades A–E*, pp. 128–132 (Cassette 7A/CD-6).

____ TWE, *Tecnotur*, Video A–B, p. 327.

____ Choose a variety of activities from the Expansion Activities Booklet.

—end of 45-minute lesson

____ Give a variety of affirmative commands. Call on students to give the negative forms.

____ Now reverse, giving the students negative commands and the students give the affirmative commands.

—end 55-minute lesson

ASSESS

____ CQ, Quizzes 3, 4, pp. 52–53.

ENRICHMENT / EXPANSION

____ Have students classify the parts of the car under one of the following 3 categories: parts necessary to drive the car, safety features, and other features.

CLOSE

____ Have students write commands for what their friends should do or not do on holidays. Jan. 1, Feb. 14, July 4, Sept. 16, Oct. 12, and Dec. 25. (Feb. 14—*Compra flores para tu novia.*)

HOMEWORK ASSIGNMENTS	TEACHER NOTES

Teacher's Name _____ Date _____

Class(es) _____ Date(s) _____ M Tu W Th F

LOCAL OBJECTIVES	**BRR:** Bell Ringer Review **TWE:** Teacher's Wraparound Edition **CQ:** Chapter Quizzes	**STM:** Student Tape Manual **WKBK:** Workbook

Chapter Objectives: The students will

- talk about cars and driving.
- give directions on the road.
- tell family and friends what to do and what not to do.
- talk about highways in the Hispanic world.

FOCUS

____ Go over any homework assignments.

____ TWE, BRR, p. 316.

TEACH

____ TWE, Teaching the Reading, *La carretera panamericana*, pp. 318–319.

____ TWE, *Después de leer A–B*, p. 319.

____ TWE, *Actividades orales A–C*, p. 324.

____ TWE, *Actividades escritas A–B*, p. 325.

—end of 45-minute lesson

____ TWE, Technology Option, p. 319.

____ TWE, Internet, p. 327.

—end of 55-minute lesson

ASSESS

____ CQ, Quiz 5, p. 54.

ENRICHMENT / EXPANSION

____ TWE, **Geography Connection**, p. 319.

____ TWE, *Lectura opcional 1*, p. 320.

____ TWE, **Learning From Realia**, p. 320.

____ TWE, *Lectura opcional 2*, p. 321.

____ TWE, **Did You Know?**, p. 321.

____ TWE, Technology Option, p. 325.

CLOSE

____ Have students write 5 commands for his/her partner to perform.

____ TWE, Writing Strategy, A–B, p. 325.

HOMEWORK ASSIGNMENTS	TEACHER NOTES

Teacher's Name _____ Date _____

Class(es) _____ Date(s) _____ M Tu W Th F

LOCAL OBJECTIVES	**BRR:** Bell Ringer Review **TWE:** Teacher's Wraparound Edition **CQ:** Chapter Quizzes	**STM:** Student Tape Manual **WKBK:** Workbook

Chapter Objectives: The students will

- talk about cars and driving.
- give directions on the road.
- tell family and friends what to do and what not to do.
- talk about highways in the Hispanic world.

FOCUS

____ Go over any homework assignments.

____ Use Vocabulary Transparencies 11.1 (A&B) and 11.2 (A&B) to review. Have students say as much as possible about the vocabulary.

____ Review Chapter Objectives, TWE, p. 300, asking students to give examples of what they have learned.

____ Complete any remaining activities from the Expansion Activities Booklet.

—*end of 45-minute lesson*

____ Show Communication Transparency C–11 and discuss with the students.

____ Use Situation Cards, *Capítulo* 11, to practice.

—*end of 55-minute lesson*

ASSESS

____ Testing Program, *Capítulo 11*, pp. 74–77, p. 136; Speaking Test p. 180; Proficiency Test pp. 200–201.

ENRICHMENT / EXPANSION

____ TWE, *Conexiones, Las ciencias*, pp. 322–323.

____ TWE, **Learning From Photos**, p. 322.

____ TWE, **Learning From Realia**, p. 323.

____ WKBK, *Act. A–E*, pp. 127–129.

CLOSE

____ TWE, *Mi autobiografía*, p. 130.

HOMEWORK ASSIGNMENTS	TEACHER NOTES

Teacher's Name _____ Date _____

Class(es) _____ Date(s) _____ M Tu W Th F

LOCAL OBJECTIVES	
	BRR: Bell Ringer Review **STM:** Student Tape Manual **TWE:** Teacher's Wraparound Edition **WKBK:** Workbook **CQ:** Chapter Quizzes
	Lesson Objectives: The students will review the vocabulary and structures from *Capítulos 8–11* and use them successfully in the *Repaso* activities.

FOCUS

_____ Go over any homework assignments.

_____ TWE, Teaching the Conversation, A–B, p. 328.

TEACH

_____ TWE, *Después de conversar A*, p. 328.

_____ TWE, Teaching Structure, *El presente perfecto*, A–B, p. 329.

_____ TWE, *Práctica A*, p. 329.

_____ TWE, Teaching Structure, *Pronombres con el participio y el infinitivo*, p. 330.

_____ TWE, *Práctica A–B*, p. 330.

_____ TWE, Teaching Structure, *Comparación de igualdad*, A–B, p. 330.

_____ TWE, *Práctica A*, p. 331.

—*end of 45-minute lesson*

_____ TWE, *Actividades comunicativas A–C*, p. 331.

—*end of 55-minute lesson*

ENRICHMENT / EXPANSION

_____ CD-ROM, Disc 3, *Juegos de repaso*, Chapters 8–11.

CLOSE

_____ WKBK, Self-Test 3, *Act. A–L*, pp. 131–136.

HOMEWORK ASSIGNMENTS	TEACHER NOTES

Teacher's Name _____ Date _____

Class(es) _____ Date(s) _____ M Tu W Th F

LOCAL OBJECTIVES	**BRR:** Bell Ringer Review **STM:** Student Tape Manual **TWE:** Teacher's Wraparound Edition **WKBK:** Workbook **CQ:** Chapter Quizzes
	Lesson Objectives: The students will review the vocabulary and structures from *Capítulos 8–11* and use them successfully in the *Repaso* activities.

FOCUS

____ Correct WKBK, Self-Test 3, *Act. A–L*, pp. 131–136.

ASSESS

____ Testing Program, Unit Test: Capítulos 8–11, pp. 78–81, p. 137; Speaking Test p. 181.

—*end of 45-minute lesson*

____ Choose one or more Tasks from Performance Assessment, Tasks 8–11, to administer in addition to or instead of the Unit Test.

—*end of 55-minute lesson*

ENRICHMENT / EXPANSION

____ TWE, **Learning From Photos**, p. 328.

____ TWE, **Learning From Photos**, p. 329.

____ TWE, **Learning From Photos**, p. 330.

CLOSE

____ TWE, *Vistas del Perú*, pp. 332–335.

HOMEWORK ASSIGNMENTS	**TEACHER NOTES**

LESSON PLANS
Copyright © Glencoe/McGraw-Hill

¡**Buen viaje! Level 2 Review Chapters 8–11** ᔕ **119**

Teacher's Name _____ Date _____

Class(es) _____ Date(s) _____ M Tu W Th F

LOCAL OBJECTIVES	
	BRR: Bell Ringer Review **STM:** Student Tape Manual **TWE:** Teacher's Wraparound Edition **WKBK:** Workbook **CQ:** Chapter Quizzes

Chapter Objectives: The students will

- talk about going to the hairdresser/barber shop.
- talk about having their clothes cleaned.
- talk about using the services of the post office and bank.
- talk about things that may or may not happen.
- express what they would like, wish, or hope others would do.

Note to teacher: For all Lesson Plan activities based on the student textbook you may use the CD-ROM version of *¡Buen viaje!* The CD-ROM is also an excellent reinforcement tool for students to use on those days when the class does not meet.

FOCUS

_____ Go over any homework assignments.

_____ Give an overview of the chapter and explain TWE, **Chapter Projects**, p. 337.

_____ TWE, BRR, p. 338.

TEACH

_____ TWE, Teaching Vocabulary, *Palabras 1,* A–E, pp. 338–339. Use STM, *Actividad A,* p. 133 (Cassette 7B/CD7).

_____ TWE, **Vocabulary Expansion**, p. 339.

_____ TWE, *Práctica A–D,* pp. 340–341.

_____ TWE, *Actividades comunicativas A–C,* p. 341.

—*end of 45-minute lesson*

_____ TWE, **Pantomime**, p. 338.

_____ TWE, **Learning From Photos**, p. 340.

—*end of 55-minute lesson*

ENRICHMENT / EXPANSION

_____ TWE, **Spotlight on Culture**, p. 337.

_____ TWE, **Did You Know?**, p. 339.

_____ TWE, Writing Development, p. 340.

_____ TWE, Technology Options, p. 341.

_____ TWE, **Learning From Photos**, p. 341.

_____ TWE, **Did You Know?**, p. 341.

CLOSE

_____ WKBK, *Act. A–E,* pp. 137–139.

Teacher's Name _____ Date _____

Class(es) _____ Date(s) _____ M Tu W Th F

LOCAL OBJECTIVES	
	BRR: Bell Ringer Review **TWE:** Teacher's Wraparound Edition **CQ:** Chapter Quizzes **STM:** Student Tape Manual **WKBK:** Workbook
	Chapter Objectives: The students will • talk about going to the hairdresser/barber shop. • talk about having their clothes cleaned. • talk about using the services of the post office and bank. • talk about things that may or may not happen. • express what they would like, wish, or hope others would do.
	FOCUS ____ Go over any homework assignments. ____ TWE, BRR, p. 342.
	TEACH ____ TWE, Teaching Vocabulary, *Palabras 2,* A–B, p. 342. Use STM, *Actividad D,* p. 135 (Cassette 7B/CD7). ____ TWE, **Vocabulary Expansion**, p. 343. ____ TWE, *Práctica A–D,* pp. 344–345. *—end of 45-minute lesson* ____ TWE, **Pantomime**, p. 342. ____ TWE, **Learning From Photos**, p. 345. *—end of 55-minute lesson*
	ENRICHMENT / EXPANSION ____ TWE, **Learning From Realia**, p. 344. ____ TWE, Technology Option, p. 345. ____ TWE, **Did You Know?**, p. 345.
	CLOSE ____ TWE, *Actividades comunicativas A–B,* p. 345. ____ WKBK, *Act. F–H,* pp. 140–141.

	HOMEWORK ASSIGNMENTS	TEACHER NOTES

Teacher's Name _____ Date _____

Class(es) _____ Date(s) _____ M Tu W Th F

LOCAL OBJECTIVES	**BRR:** Bell Ringer Review **TWE:** Teacher's Wraparound Edition **CQ:** Chapter Quizzes	**STM:** Student Tape Manual **WKBK:** Workbook

Chapter Objectives: The students will

- talk about going to the hairdresser/barber shop.
- talk about having their clothes cleaned.
- talk about using the services of the post office and bank.
- talk about things that may or may not happen.
- express what they would like, wish, or hope others would do.

FOCUS

_____ Go over any homework assignments.

_____ TWE, BRR, p. 346.

TEACH

_____ STM, *Actividades B-C*, p. 134, *E-G*, pp. 136–137 (Cassette 7B/CD7).

_____ TWE, Teaching Structure, *El subjuntivo*, A–D, pp. 346–347.

_____ TWE, *Práctica A–B*, p. 348.

_____ Have students give each other indirect commands to perform. (*Juan, quiero que escribas tu nombre en la pizarra. María, insisto en que cierres la puerta.*)

—*end of 45-minute lesson*

_____ Give the students direct commands and indirect commands so that they can hear the difference. (*Juan, abre la puerta. Juan, quiero que abras la puerta.*)

_____ Write an indirect command leaving blanks for students to fill in. (_____ (name of student), *quiero que* _____. _____ (name), *espero que* _____.)

—*end of 55-minute lesson*

ASSESS

_____ CQ, Quizzes 1, 2, pp. 55–56.

ENRICHMENT / EXPANSION

_____ TWE, **Fine Art Connection**, p. 346.

CLOSE

_____ WKBK, *Act A*, p. 142.

HOMEWORK ASSIGNMENTS	TEACHER NOTES

Teacher's Name _____ Date _____

Class(es) _____ Date(s) _____ M Tu W Th F

LOCAL OBJECTIVES	**BRR:** Bell Ringer Review **TWE:** Teacher's Wraparound Edition **CQ:** Chapter Quizzes	**STM:** Student Tape Manual **WKBK:** Workbook

Chapter Objectives: The students will

- talk about going to the hairdresser/barber shop.
- talk about having their clothes cleaned.
- talk about using the services of the post office and bank.
- talk about things that may or may not happen.
- express what they would like, wish, or hope others would do.

FOCUS

____ Go over any homework assignments.

____ TWE, BRR, p. 351.

TEACH

____ TWE, Teaching Structure, *El subjuntivo en cláusulas nominales*, p. 349.

____ TWE, *Práctica A–E*, pp. 349–350.

____ TWE, *Actividades comunicativas A–B*, p. 351.

____ STM, *Actividades A–B*, pp. 137–138 (Cassette 7B/CD7).

—end of 45-minute lesson

____ TWE, **Learning From Realia**, p. 347.

____ Have students complete the following statements: *Mi mejor amigo quiere que yo... Mis padres temen que mis hermanos... Mis abuelos insisten en que yo... Yo deseo que mis amigos... La maestra tiene miedo de que los alumnos... El jefe manda que los empleados...*

—end of 55-minute lesson

ENRICHMENT / EXPANSION

____ TWE, **Learning From Photos**, p. 348.

CLOSE

____ WKBK, *Act. B–E*, pp. 143–145.

HOMEWORK ASSIGNMENTS	TEACHER NOTES

Teacher's Name _____ Date _____

Class(es) _____ Date(s) _____ M Tu W Th F

LOCAL OBJECTIVES	**BRR:** Bell Ringer Review **STM:** Student Tape Manual
	TWE: Teacher's Wraparound Edition **WKBK:** Workbook
	CQ: Chapter Quizzes

Chapter Objectives: The students will

- talk about going to the hairdresser/barber shop.
- talk about having their clothes cleaned.
- talk about using the services of the post office and bank.
- talk about things that may or may not happen.
- express what they would like, wish, or hope others would do.

FOCUS

____ Go over any homework assignments.

____ TWE, **Learning From Realia**, p. 351.

TEACH

____ TWE, Teaching Structure, *El subjuntivo con expresiones impersonales*, p. 351

____ TWE, *Práctica A–D*, pp. 352–353.

____ TWE, *Actividad comunicativa A*, p. 353.

____ STM, *Actividades C-D*, pp. 138–139 (Cassette 7B/CD7).

—end of 45-minute lesson

____ Make up original statements and have the class determine if each statement is true or false. (*Es posible que haya clases los sábados. Es probable que el presidente de los Estados Unidos visite nuestra ciudad.*)

—end of 55-minute lesson

ASSESS

____ CQ, Quiz 3, p. 57.

ENRICHMENT / EXPANSION

____ TWE, **Learning From Realia**, p. 349.

____ TWE, **Learning From Realia**, p. 352.

____ TWE, **Learning From Realia**, p. 353.

CLOSE

____ TWE, *Juego*, p. 353.

____ WKBK, *Act. F–H*, pp. 145–146.

HOMEWORK ASSIGNMENTS	TEACHER NOTES

Teacher's Name _____ Date _____

Class(es) _____ Date(s) _____ M Tu W Th F

LOCAL OBJECTIVES	**BRR:** Bell Ringer Review **TWE:** Teacher's Wraparound Edition **CQ:** Chapter Quizzes	**STM:** Student Tape Manual **WKBK:** Workbook

Chapter Objectives: The students will

- talk about going to the hairdresser/barber shop.
- talk about having their clothes cleaned.
- talk about using the services of the post office and bank.
- talk about things that may or may not happen.
- express what they would like, wish, or hope others would do.

FOCUS

____ Go over any homework assignments.

____ TWE, BRR, p. 354.

TEACH

____ TWE, Teaching the Conversation, A–E, p. 354. Use STM, *Actividades E-F,* p. 140 (Cassette 7B/CD7).

____ TWE, *Después de conversar A,* p. 354.

____ TWE, *Tecnotur,* Video A–B, p. 365.

____ TWE, *Actividades comunicativas A–B,* p. 355.

—*end of 45-minute lesson*

____ Choose a variety of activities from the Expansion Activities Booklet.

—*end of 55-minute lesson*

ASSESS

____ CQ, Quizzes 4, 5, pp. 58–59.

ENRICHMENT / EXPANSION

____ TWE, Technology Option, p. 355.

____ TWE, **Learning from Photos**, p. 355.

____ TWE, **Geography Connection**, p. 355.

____ TWE, *Lectura opcional 1,* p. 358.

____ TWE, **Did You Know?**, p. 358.

CLOSE

____ STM, *Actividades A–C,* pp. 141–144 (Cassette 7B/CD7).

HOMEWORK ASSIGNMENTS	TEACHER NOTES

Teacher's Name _____ Date _____

Class(es) _____ Date(s) _____ M Tu W Th F

LOCAL OBJECTIVES	**BRR:** Bell Ringer Review **STM:** Student Tape Manual
	TWE: Teacher's Wraparound Edition **WKBK:** Workbook
	CQ: Chapter Quizzes

Chapter Objectives: The students will

- talk about going to the hairdresser/barbershop.
- talk about having their clothes cleaned.
- talk about using the services of the post office and bank.
- talk about things that may or may not happen.
- express what they would like, wish, or hope others would do.

FOCUS

_____ Go over any homework assignments.

_____ TWE, BRR, p. 356.

TEACH

_____ TWE, Teaching the Reading, *Muchos quehaceres*, pp. 356–357.

_____ TWE, *Después de leer A–B*, p. 357.

_____ TWE, *Actividades orales A–C*, p. 362.

_____ TWE, *Actividad escrita A*, p. 363.

—*end of 45-minute lesson*

_____ TWE, Technology Option, p. 363.

—*end of 55-minute lesson*

ENRICHMENT / EXPANSION

_____ TWE, Technology Option, p. 357.

_____ TWE, **Learning From Photos**, p. 357.

_____ TWE, *Lectura opcional 2*, p. 359.

_____ TWE, **Learning From Photos**, p. 359.

_____ TWE, **Learning From Photos**, p. 363.

CLOSE

_____ TWE, Writing Strategy, A–B, p. 363.

HOMEWORK ASSIGNMENTS	TEACHER NOTES

Teacher's Name _____ Date _____

Class(es) _____ Date(s) _____ M Tu W Th F

LOCAL OBJECTIVES	**BRR:** Bell Ringer Review **TWE:** Teacher's Wraparound Edition **CQ:** Chapter Quizzes	**STM:** Student Tape Manual **WKBK:** Workbook

Chapter Objectives: The students will

• talk about going to the hairdresser/barber shop.

• talk about having their clothes cleaned.

• talk about using the services of the post office and bank.

• talk about things that may or may not happen.

• express what they would like, wish, or hope others would do.

FOCUS

_____ Go over any homework assignments.

_____ Use Vocabulary Transparencies 12.1 (A&B) and 12.2 (A&B) to review. Have students say as much as possible about the vocabulary.

_____ Review Chapter Objectives, TWE, p. 336, asking students to give examples of what they have learned.

_____ Choose any remaining activities from the Expansion Activities Booklet.

—end of 45-minute lesson

_____ Show Communication Transparency C–12 and discuss with the students.

_____ Use Situation Cards, *Capítulo 12,* to practice.

—end of 55-minute lesson

ASSESS

_____ Testing Program, *Capítulo 12,* pp. 82–86, p. 138; Speaking Test, p. 182, Proficiency Test p. 202.

ENRICHMENT / EXPANSION

_____ TWE, *Conexiones, Las finanzas,* pp. 360–361.

_____ TWE, **About the Spanish Language**, p. 360.

_____ TWE, **Career Connection**, p. 361.

_____ TWE, Internet, p. 365.

_____ WKBK, *Act. A–E,* pp. 147–149.

CLOSE

_____ WKBK, *Mi autobiografía,* p. 150.

	HOMEWORK ASSIGNMENTS	**TEACHER NOTES**

Teacher's Name _____ Date _____

Class(es) _____ Date(s) _____ M Tu W Th F

LOCAL OBJECTIVES	
	BRR: Bell Ringer Review **STM:** Student Tape Manual **TWE:** Teacher's Wraparound Edition **WKBK:** Workbook **CQ:** Chapter Quizzes

Chapter Objectives: The students will

- describe and talk about parties and weddings.
- talk about some holidays.
- give advice and make recommendations.
- express doubt, uncertainty, or disbelief.
- express emotional reactions to what others do.
- talk about New Year's Eve in the Hispanic world.

Note to teacher: For all Lesson Plan activities based on the student textbook you may use the CD-ROM version of *¡Buen viaje!* The CD-ROM is also an excellent reinforcement tool for students to use on those days when the class does not meet.

FOCUS

____ Go over any homework assignments.

____ Give an overview of the chapter and explain TWE, **Chapter Projects**, p. 367.

____ TWE, BRR, p. 368.

TEACH

____ TWE, Teaching Vocabulary, *Palabras 1*, A–B, p. 368. Use STM, *Actividad A*, p. 145 (Cassette 8A/CD7).

____ TWE, Recycling, p. 369.

____ TWE, *Práctica A–C*, pp. 370–371.

____ TWE, *Actividades comunicativas A–B*, p. 371.

—*end of 45-minute lesson*

____ TWE, **Learning From Realia**, p. 371.

____ TWE, Expansion, *Práctica A–B*, p. 370.

—*end of 55-minute lesson*

ENRICHMENT / EXPANSION

____ TWE, **Spotlight on Culture**, p. 367.

____ TWE, **Did You Know?**, p. 369.

____ TWE, Writing Development, p. 370.

____ TWE, Technology Option, p. 371.

CLOSE

____ TWE, **Pantomime**, p. 368.

____ WKBK, *Act. A–C*, pp. 151–152.

Teacher's Name _____ Date _____

Class(es) _____ Date(s) _____ M Tu W Th F

LOCAL OBJECTIVES	**BRR:** Bell Ringer Review **TWE:** Teacher's Wraparound Edition **CQ:** Chapter Quizzes	**STM:** Student Tape Manual **WKBK:** Workbook

Chapter Objectives: The students will

- describe and talk about parties and weddings.
- talk about some holidays.
- give advice and make recommendations.
- express doubt, uncertainty, or disbelief.
- express emotional reactions to what others do.
- talk about New Year's Eve in the Hispanic world.

FOCUS

____ Go over any homework assignments.

____ TWE, BRR, p. 372.

TEACH

____ TWE, Teaching Vocabulary, *Palabras 2*, A–B, p. 372. Use STM, *Actividad D*, p. 147 (Cassette 8A/CD7).

____ TWE, **Vocabulary Expansion**, p. 373.

____ TWE, *Práctica A–C*, pp. 374–375.

____ TWE, *Actividades comunicativas A–B*, p. 375.

—*end of 45-minute lesson*

____ Preview TWE, *Palabras 1*, pp. 368–369. Ask students to work in small groups to discuss what particular events happened in their families relating to either of the situations presented in the pictures. Select a recorder for the group who will take notes and report to the class.

____ Hold a class discussion related to food for each of the events in *Palabras 1*. Which foods are part of these celebrations?

—*end of 55-minute lesson*

ENRICHMENT / EXPANSION

____ TWE, **Did You Know?**, p. 373.

____ TWE, Expansion, *Práctica B*, p. 374.

____ TWE, Writing Development, p. 374.

____ TWE, Writing Development, p. 375.

____ TWE, Technology Option, p. 375.

CLOSE

____ WKBK, *Act. D–F*, pp. 153–154.

Teacher's Name _____ Date _____

Class(es) _____ Date(s) _____ M Tu W Th F

LOCAL OBJECTIVES	**BRR:** Bell Ringer Review **STM:** Student Tape Manual
	TWE: Teacher's Wraparound Edition **WKBK:** Workbook
	CQ: Chapter Quizzes

Chapter Objectives: The students will

- describe and talk about parties and weddings.
- talk about some holidays.
- give advice and make recommendations.
- express doubt, uncertainty, or disbelief.
- express emotional reactions to what others do.
- talk about New Year's Eve in the Hispanic world.

FOCUS

____ Go over any homework assignments.

____ TWE, BRR, p. 376.

TEACH

____ STM, *Actividades B–C*, p. 146, *E–F*, pp. 148–149 (Cassette 8A/CD7).

____ TWE, Teaching Structure, *El subjuntivo de los verbos de cambio radical*, A–D, p. 376. Use the impersonal expressions and model by using a combination of these and the stem-changing verbs. (*Es imposible que los Dallas Cowboys pierden el juego. Espero que no te duermas en el concierto.*) Call on volunteers to make up some statements.

____ TWE, *Práctica A–B*, p. 377.

—*end of 45-minute lesson*

____ TWE, Expansion, *Práctica A*, p. 377.

____ TWE, Writing Development, p. 377.

—*end of 55-minute lesson*

ASSESS

____ CQ, Quizzes 1, 2, pp. 60–61

ENRICHMENT / EXPANSION

____ TWE, **Learning From Realia**, p. 377.

CLOSE

____ WKBK, *Act. A*, p. 155.

HOMEWORK ASSIGNMENTS	TEACHER NOTES

Teacher's Name _____ Date _____

Class(es) _____ Date(s) _____ M Tu W Th F

LOCAL OBJECTIVES	**BRR:** Bell Ringer Review **TWE:** Teacher's Wraparound Edition **CQ:** Chapter Quizzes	**STM:** Student Tape Manual **WKBK:** Workbook

Chapter Objectives: The students will

- describe and talk about parties and weddings.
- talk about some holidays.
- give advice and make recommendations.
- express doubt, uncertainty, or disbelief.
- express emotional reactions to what others do.
- talk about New Year's Eve in the Hispanic world.

FOCUS

____ Go over any homework assignments.

____ TWE, BRR, p. 378.

TEACH

____ TWE, Teaching Structure, *El subjuntivo con verbos como* **pedir** *y* **aconsejar**, A–C, p. 378.

____ TWE, *Práctica A–D*, pp. 378–379.

____ Ask choice questions using the new verbs. For example: *¿Sugieres que la clase tome el examen el jueves o el viernes? Recomiendas que comamos en el restaurante _____ o _____?* Ask as many questions as possible using the new verbs.

____ STM, *Actividad A*, p. 150 (Cassette 8A/CD7).

—*end of 45-minute lesson*

____ TWE, Expansion, *Práctica A*, p. 378.

____ TWE, Expansion, *Práctica C*, p. 379.

—*end of 55-minute lesson*

ENRICHMENT / EXPANSION

____ TWE, **Learning From Photos**, p. 378.

____ TWE, **Learning From Realia**, p. 379.

CLOSE

____ TWE, *Actividad comunicativa A*, p. 379.

____ WKBK, *Act. B–C*, pp. 156–157.

HOMEWORK ASSIGNMENTS	TEACHER NOTES

Teacher's Name _____ Date _____

Class(es) _____ Date(s) _____ M Tu W Th F

LOCAL OBJECTIVES	**BRR:** Bell Ringer Review **TWE:** Teacher's Wraparound Edition **CQ:** Chapter Quizzes	**STM:** Student Tape Manual **WKBK:** Workbook

Chapter Objectives: The students will

- describe and talk about parties and weddings.
- talk about some holidays.
- give advice and make recommendations.
- express doubt, uncertainty, or disbelief.
- express emotional reactions to what others do.
- talk about New Year's Eve in the Hispanic world.

FOCUS

_____ Go over any homework assignments.

_____ TWE, BRR, p. 380.

TEACH

_____ TWE, Teaching Structure, *El subjuntivo con expresiones de duda,* A–B, p. 380.

_____ TWE, *Práctica A–C,* pp. 380–381.

_____ TWE, *Actividad comunicativa A,* p. 381.

_____ TWE, Teaching Structure, *El subjuntivo con expresiones de emoción,* A–B, p. 382.

_____ TWE, *Práctica A–C,* p. 382–383.

_____ TWE, *Actividad comunicativa A,* p. 383.

—end of 45-minute lesson

_____ Have students work in pairs to express statements of doubt and uncertainty about the following situation: The Spanish class was supposed to go on a field trip today to _____ and do several activities there; however, it has just started raining and the bus has not arrived. (*Dudo que vayamos a _____. No creo que comamos en el restaurante.*)

—end of 55-minute lesson

ENRICHMENT / EXPANSION

_____ TWE, **Learning From Realia**, p. 380.

_____ TWE, **Critical Thinking Activity**, p. 381.

_____ TWE, **Learning From Photos**, p. 382.

CLOSE

_____ WKBK, *Act. D–F,* pp. 158–159.

HOMEWORK ASSIGNMENTS	TEACHER NOTES

Teacher's Name _____ Date _____

Class(es) _____ Date(s) _____ M Tu W Th F

LOCAL OBJECTIVES	**BRR:** Bell Ringer Review **STM:** Student Tape Manual **TWE:** Teacher's Wraparound Edition **WKBK:** Workbook **CQ:** Chapter Quizzes
	Chapter Objectives: The students will • describe and talk about parties and weddings. • talk about some holidays. • give advice and make recommendations. • express doubt, uncertainty, or disbelief. • express emotional reactions to what others do. • talk about New Year's Eve in the Hispanic world.

FOCUS
____ Go over any homework assignments.
____ TWE, BRR, p. 384.

TEACH
____ STM, *Actividades B–D*, pp. 150–152 (Cassette 8A/CD7).
____ TWE, Teaching the Conversation, A–F, p. 384. Use STM, *Actividades E–F*, p. 153 (Cassette 8A/CD7).
____ TWE, *Después de conversar*, p. 384.
____ TWE, *Actividades comunicativas A–B*, p. 385.
____ STM, *Actividades A–D*, pp. 154–156 (Cassette 8A/CD7).
____ TWE, *Tecnotur*, Video A–B, p. 395.
____ Have students write a paragraph of 7–10 sentences telling why they are happy or sad. After a given period of time, have the students exchange papers. They will read the paragraph and write comments expressing that they are happy or sad for the other students.
—end of 45-minute lesson
____ Have students generate a list of school events or other personal events for which they are happy or sad. Ask students to express their emotions about these events. (*Me alegro que nuestro equipo haya ganado el partido de fútbol. Es una lástima que Julio se haya roto la pierna.*)
—end of 55-minute lesson

ASSESS
____ CQ, Quizzes 3, 4, pp. 62–63.

ENRICHMENT / EXPANSION
____ TWE, Technology Option, p. 384.
____ TWE, **Did You Know?**, p. 385.
____ TWE, *Lectura opcional 1*, p. 388.
____ TWE, **Learning From Photos**, p. 388.

CLOSE
____ Have students make statements related to the festivities in *Palabras 1* or *Palabras 2*. (*Es necesario que compres todos los regalos antes del día 15 de diciembre. Es posible que vayamos a Denver para la Navidad.*)

LEVEL 2 LESSON PLAN CHAPTER 13: DAY 7

Teacher's Name _____ Date _____

Class(es) _____ Date(s) _____ M Tu W Th F

LOCAL OBJECTIVES	**BRR:** Bell Ringer Review **STM:** Student Tape Manual **TWE:** Teacher's Wraparound Edition **WKBK:** Workbook **CQ:** Chapter Quizzes

Chapter Objectives: The students will

- describe and talk about parties and weddings.
- talk about some holidays.
- give advice and make recommendations.
- express doubt, uncertainty, or disbelief.
- express emotional reactions to what others do.
- talk about New Year's Eve in the Hispanic world.

FOCUS

_____ Go over any homework assignments.

_____ TWE, BRR, p. 386.

TEACH

_____ TWE, Teaching the Reading, *Las doce uvas de la felicidad*, p. 386.

_____ TWE, *Después de leer A–B,* p. 387.

_____ TWE, *Actividades orales A–C,* p. 392.

_____ TWE, *Actividades escritas A–B,* p. 393.

_____ Choose a variety of activities from the Expansion Activities Booklet.

—end of 45-minute lesson

_____ TWE, Paired Activity, p. 392.

_____ TWE, Technology Option, p. 393.

—end of 55-minute lesson

ASSESS

_____ CQ, Quizzes 5, 6, pp. 64–65.

ENRICHMENT / EXPANSION

_____ TWE, **Learning From Photos**, p. 386.

_____ TWE, **Did You Know?**, p. 386.

_____ TWE, Technology Option, p. 387.

_____ TWE, **History Connection**, p. 387.

_____ TWE, *Lectura opcional 2,* p. 389.

_____ TWE, **Did You Know?**, p. 389.

_____ TWE, Technology Option, p. 392.

CLOSE

_____ TWE, Writing Strategy, A–B, p. 393.

Teacher's Name _____ Date _____

Class(es) _____ Date(s) _____ M Tu W Th F

LOCAL OBJECTIVES	**BRR:** Bell Ringer Review **TWE:** Teacher's Wraparound Edition **CQ:** Chapter Quizzes	**STM:** Student Tape Manual **WKBK:** Workbook

Chapter Objectives: The students will

- describe and talk about parties and weddings.
- talk about some holidays.
- give advice and make recommendations.
- express doubt, uncertainty, or disbelief.
- express emotional reactions to what others do.
- talk about New Year's Eve in the Hispanic world.

FOCUS

____ Go over any homework assignments.

____ Use Vocabulary Transparencies 13.1 (A&B) and 13.2 (A&B) to review. Have students say as much as possible about the vocabulary.

____ Review Chapter Objectives, TWE, p. 366, asking students to give examples of what they have learned.

____ Complete any remaining activities from the Expansion Activities Booklet.

—*end of 45-minute lesson*

____ Show Communication Transparency C–13 and discuss with the students.

____ Use Situation Cards, *Capítulo 13*, to practice.

—*end of 55-minute lesson*

ASSESS

____ Testing Program, *Capítulo 13*, pp. 87–90, p. 139; Speaking Test p. 183; Proficiency Test p. 203.

ENRICHMENT / EXPANSION

____ TWE, *Conexiones, Las bellas artes*, pp. 390–391.

____ TWE, **Did You Know?**, p. 390.

____ TWE, Internet, p. 395.

____ WKBK, *Act. A-H*, pp. 160–163.

CLOSE

____ TWE, *Mi autobiografía*, p. 164.

HOMEWORK ASSIGNMENTS	TEACHER NOTES

Teacher's Name _____ Date _____

Class(es) _____ Date(s) _____ M Tu W Th F

LOCAL OBJECTIVES	**BRR:** Bell Ringer Review **TWE:** Teacher's Wraparound Edition **CQ:** Chapter Quizzes	**STM:** Student Tape Manual **WKBK:** Workbook

Chapter Objectives: The students will

- talk about professions and occupations.
- interview for a job.
- state work qualifications.
- talk about future events.
- talk about probable events.

Note to teacher: For all Lesson Plan activities based on the student textbook you may use the CD-ROM version of *¡Buen viaje!* The CD-ROM is also an excellent reinforcement tool for students to use on those days when the class does not meet.

FOCUS

____ Go over any homework assignments.

____ Give an overview of the chapter and explain TWE, **Chapter Projects**, p. 397.

____ TWE, BRR, p. 398.

TEACH

____ TWE, Teaching Vocabulary, *Palabras 1*, A–C, p. 398. Use STM, *Actividad A*, p. 157 (Cassette 8B/CD8) and Vocabulary Transparencies 14.1 (A&B).

____ TWE, **About the Spanish Language**, p. 399.

____ TWE, *Práctica A–D*, pp. 400–401.

____ TWE, **Learning From Realia**, p. 401.

____ TWE, *Actividad comunicativa A*, p. 401.

—*end of 45-minute lesson*

____ TWE, **Learning From Photos**, p. 398.

____ TWE, **Pantomime**, p. 398.

—*end of 55-minute lesson*

ENRICHMENT / EXPANSION

____ TWE, **Spotlight on Culture**, p. 397.

____ TWE, **Vocabulary Expansion**, p. 397.

____ TWE, Technology Option, p. 401.

CLOSE

____ TWE, *Juego*, p. 401.

____ WKBK, *Act. A–C*, pp. 165–166.

Teacher's Name _____ Date _____

Class(es) _____ Date(s) _____ M Tu W Th F

LOCAL OBJECTIVES	**BRR:** Bell Ringer Review **TWE:** Teacher's Wraparound Edition **CQ:** Chapter Quizzes	**STM:** Student Tape Manual **WKBK:** Workbook

Chapter Objectives: The students will

- talk about professions and occupations.
- interview for a job.
- state work qualifications.
- talk about future events.
- talk about probable events.

FOCUS

____ Go over any homework assignments.

____ TWE, BRR, p. 402.

____ TWE, Expansion, *Práctica B,* p. 400.

TEACH

____ TWE, Teaching Vocabulary , *Palabras 2,* A–B, pp. 402-403. Use STM, *Actividad D,* p. 159, (Cassette 9B/CD-9) and Vocabulary Transparencies 14.2 (A–B).

____ TWE, *Práctica A–C,* pp. 404-405.

____ TWE, *Actividades comunicativas A–B,* p. 405.

—end of 45-minute lesson

____ TWE, Paired Activity, p. 403.

____ TWE, **Pantomime**, p. 403.

—end of 55-minute lesson

ENRICHMENT / EXPANSION

____ TWE, **Did You Know?**, p. 402.

____ TWE, Expansion, *Práctica A–C,* p. 404.

____ TWE, Writing Development, p. 405.

____ TWE, Technology Option, p. 405.

CLOSE

____ TWE, **Learning From Realia**, p. 404.

____ WKBK, *Act. D-F,* pp. 166–167.

HOMEWORK ASSIGNMENTS	TEACHER NOTES

Teacher's Name _____ Date _____

Class(es) _____ Date(s) _____ M Tu W Th F

LOCAL OBJECTIVES	
	BRR: Bell Ringer Review **STM:** Student Tape Manual **TWE:** Teacher's Wraparound Edition **WKBK:** Workbook **CQ:** Chapter Quizzes

Chapter Objectives: The students will

- talk about professions and occupations.
- interview for a job.
- state work qualifications.
- talk about future events.
- talk about probable events.

FOCUS

_____ Go over any homework assignments.

_____ TWE, BRR, p. 406.

TEACH

_____ STM, *Actividades B-C*, pp. 158–159, *E–F*, p. 160 (Cassette 8B/CD8).

_____ TWE, Teaching Structure, *Infinitivo o subjuntivo*, A–B, p. 406.

_____ TWE, *Práctica A–C*, pp. 406–407.

—*end of 45-minute lesson*

_____ Students play vocabulary bingo using the TWE, *Vocabulario*, p. 420.

_____ Students write 10 original sentences choosing from TWE, *Palabras 1*, and *Palabras 2*.

—*end of 55-minute lesson*

ASSESS

_____ CQ, Quizzes 1, 2, pp. 66–67.

ENRICHMENT/EXPANSION

_____ TWE, **Learning From Photos**, p. 406.

_____ TWE, **Learning From Photos**, p. 407.

CLOSE

_____ TWE, *Actividad comunicativas A*, p. 409.

_____ WKBK, *Act. A*, p. 168.

HOMEWORK ASSIGNMENTS	TEACHER NOTES

Teacher's Name _____ Date _____

Class(es) _____ Date(s) _____ M Tu W Th F

LOCAL OBJECTIVES	**BRR:** Bell Ringer Review **TWE:** Teacher's Wraparound Edition **CQ:** Chapter Quizzes	**STM:** Student Tape Manual **WKBK:** Workbook

Chapter Objectives: The students will

- talk about professions and occupations.
- interview for a job.
- state work qualifications.
- talk about future events.
- talk about probable events.

FOCUS

____ Go over any homework assignments.

____ TWE, BRR, p. 408.

TEACH

____ TWE, Teaching Structure, *El subjuntivo con* **ojalá** *y* **quizá(s)**, A–B, p. 408.

____ TWE, *Práctica A–B,* p. 408.

____ TWE, Teaching Structure, *El subjuntivo en cláusulas relativas,* A–B, p. 409.

____ TWE, *Práctica A–B,* p. 409.

____ STM, *Actividades A–E,* pp. 161–163 (Cassette 8B/CD8).

—end of 45-minute lesson

____ Choose a variety of activities from the Expansion Activities Booklet.

—end of 55-minute lesson

ENRICHMENT/EXPANSION

____ TWE, **Learning From Realia**, p. 408.

____ TWE, **Learning From Realia**, p. 409.

CLOSE

____ TWE, *Actividad comunicativa A,* p. 409.

____ WKBK, *Act. B–F,* pp. 168–170.

HOMEWORK ASSIGNMENTS	TEACHER NOTES

Teacher's Name _____ Date _____

Class(es) _____ Date(s) _____ M Tu W Th F

LOCAL OBJECTIVES	
	BRR: Bell Ringer Review **STM:** Student Tape Manual **TWE:** Teacher's Wraparound Edition **WKBK:** Workbook **CQ:** Chapter Quizzes
	Chapter Objectives: The students will • talk about professions and occupations. • interview for a job. • state work qualifications. • talk about future events. • talk about probable events.
	FOCUS ____ Go over any homework assignments. ____ TWE, BRR, p. 409.
	TEACH ____ TWE, Teaching the Conversation, A–D, p. 410. Use STM, *Actividades F–G*, pp. 163–164 (Cassette 8B/CD8). ____ TWE, *Después de conversar*, p. 410. ____ TWE, *Actividades comunicativas A–C*, p. 411. ____ STM, *Actividades A–C*, pp. 164–167 (Cassette 8B/CD8). —*end of 45-minute lesson* ____ TWE, Technology Option, p. 410. —*end of 55-minute lesson*
	ASSESS ____ CQ, Quizzes 3, 4, pp. 68–69.
	ENRICHMENT / EXPANSION ____ TWE, **About the Spanish Language**, p. 411.
	CLOSE ____ TWE, **Learning From Photos**, p. 411.

HOMEWORK ASSIGNMENTS	TEACHER NOTES

Teacher's Name _____ Date _____

Class(es) _____ Date(s) _____ M Tu W Th F

LOCAL OBJECTIVES	**BRR:** Bell Ringer Review **TWE:** Teacher's Wraparound Edition **CQ:** Chapter Quizzes	**STM:** Student Tape Manual **WKBK:** Workbook

Chapter Objectives: The students will

- talk about professions and occupations.
- interview for a job.
- state work qualifications.
- talk about future events.
- talk about probable events.

FOCUS

____ Go over any homework assignments.

____ TWE, BRR, p. 412.

TEACH

____ TWE, Teaching the Reading, *Un muchacho que se llama Bobby*, pp. 412–413.

____ TWE, *Después de leer A*, p. 413.

____ Supply the students with a mock or real application for employment in Spanish. Students fill out and then exchange their application with another student. They will interview each other using the information in the application.

—*end of 45-minute lesson*

____ TWE, **Learning From Photos**, p. 412.

____ TWE, Technology Option, p. 413.

—*end of 55-minute lesson*

ENRICHMENT / EXPANSION

____ TWE, *Lectura opcional 1*, p. 414.

____ TWE, **About the Spanish Language**, p. 414.

____ TWE, **Career Connection**, p. 414.

____ TWE, **Learning From Realia**, p. 414.

____ TWE, *Lectura opcional 2*, p. 415.

CLOSE

____ TWE, **Did You Know?**, p. 412.

____ TWE, **Career Connection**, p. 413.

HOMEWORK ASSIGNMENTS	TEACHER NOTES

Teacher's Name _____ Date _____

Class(es) _____ Date(s) _____ M Tu W Th F

LOCAL OBJECTIVES	
	BRR: Bell Ringer Review **STM:** Student Tape Manual **TWE:** Teacher's Wraparound Edition **WKBK:** Workbook **CQ:** Chapter Quizzes

Chapter Objectives: The students will

- talk about professions and occupations.
- interview for a job.
- state work qualifications.
- talk about future events.
- talk about probable events.

FOCUS

_____ Go over any homework assignments.

_____ Use Vocabulary Transparencies 14.1 (A&B) and 14.2 (A&B) to review. Have students say as much as possible about the vocabulary.

TEACH

_____ TWE, *Tecnotur*, Video A–B, p. 421.

_____ TWE, *Actividades comunicativas A–D*, p. 418.

_____ TWE, *Actividades escritas A–B*, p. 419.

—end of 45-minute lesson

_____ TWE, **Learning from Photos**, p. 418.

_____ TWE, **Learning from Photos**, p. 419.

—end of 55-minute lesson

ENRICHMENT / EXPANSION

_____ TWE, Technology Option, p. 419.

_____ TWE, Internet, p. 421.

CLOSE

_____ WKBK, *Mi autobiografía*, p. 171.

HOMEWORK ASSIGNMENTS	TEACHER NOTES

Teacher's Name _____ Date _____

Class(es) _____ Date(s) _____ M Tu W Th F

LOCAL OBJECTIVES	**BRR:** Bell Ringer Review **TWE:** Teacher's Wraparound Edition **CQ:** Chapter Quizzes	**STM:** Student Tape Manual **WKBK:** Workbook

Chapter Objectives: The students will

- talk about professions and occupations.
- interview for a job.
- state work qualifications.
- talk about future events.
- talk about probable events.

FOCUS

____ Go over any homework assignments.

____ Review Chapter Objectives, TWE, p. 396, asking students to give examples of what they have learned.

____ Complete any remaining activities from the Expansion Activities Booklet.

—*end of 45-minute lesson*

____ Show Communication Transparency C–14 and discuss with the students.

____ Use Situation Cards, *Capítulo 14*, to practice. Students present the situation they have prepared with a partner.

—*end of 55-minute lesson*

ASSESS

____ Testing Program, *Capítulo 14*, pp. 91–94, p. 140; Speaking Test p. 184; Proficiency Test p. 205.

ENRICHMENT / EXPANSION

____ WKBK, *Ej. A–E*, pp. 171–173.

____ TWE, *Conexiones, Las ciencias sociales*, pp. 416–417.

____ TWE, **Critical Thinking Activity**, p. 416.

____ TWE, **Did You Know?**, p. 417.

CLOSE

____ TWE, Writing Strategy, A–B, p. 419.

HOMEWORK ASSIGNMENTS	TEACHER NOTES

Teacher's Name _____ Date _____

Class(es) _____ Date(s) _____ M Tu W Th F

LOCAL OBJECTIVES		
	BRR: Bell Ringer Review	**STM:** Student Tape Manual
	TWE: Teacher's Wraparound Edition	**WKBK:** Workbook
	CQ: Chapter Quizzes	

Lesson Objectives: The students will review the vocabulary and structures from *Capítulos 12–14* and use them successfully in the *Repaso* activities.

FOCUS

____ Go over any homework assignments.

____ TWE, Teaching the Conversation, A–B, p. 422.

TEACH

____ TWE, *Después de conversar A*, p. 422.

____ TWE, Teaching Structure, *Usos del subjuntivo*, A–B, p. 423.

____ TWE, *Práctica A–C*, pp. 423–424.

____ TWE, Teaching Structure, *Más usos del subjuntivo*, A–B, p. 424.

____ TWE, *Práctica A–B*, p. 425.

—*end of 45-minute lesson*

____ TWE, *Actividades comunicativas A–C*, p. 425.

—*end of 55-minute lesson*

ENRICHMENT / EXPANSION

____ TWE, CD-ROM, Disc 4, *Juegos de repaso*, Chapters 12–14.

CLOSE

____ WKBK, Self-Test 4, *Act. A–I*, pp. 175–178.

HOMEWORK ASSIGNMENTS	TEACHER NOTES

Teacher's Name _____ Date _____

Class(es) _____ Date(s) _____ M Tu W Th F

LOCAL OBJECTIVES	
	BRR: Bell Ringer Review **STM:** Student Tape Manual **TWE:** Teacher's Wraparound Edition **WKBK:** Workbook **CQ:** Chapter Quizzes
	Lesson Objectives: The students will review the vocabulary and structures from *Capítulos 12–14* and use them successfully in the *Repaso* activities.
	FOCUS ____ Correct WKBK, Self-Test 4, *Act. A–I*, pp. 175–178.
	ASSESS ____ Testing Program, Unit Test: Capítulos 12–14, pp. 95–98, p. 141; Speaking Test p. 185. —*end of 45-minute lesson* ____ Choose one or more Tasks from Performance Assessment, Tasks 12–14, to administer in addition to or instead of the Unit Test. —*end of 55-minute lesson*
	CLOSE ____ TWE, *Vistas de Guatemala*, pp. 426–429.

	HOMEWORK ASSIGNMENTS	TEACHER NOTES

Teacher's Name _____ Date _____

Class(es) _____ Date(s) _____ M Tu W Th F

LOCAL OBJECTIVES	**BRR:** Bell Ringer Review **TWE:** Teacher's Wraparound Edition **CQ:** Chapter Quizzes	**STM:** Student Tape Manual **WKBK:** Workbook

HOMEWORK ASSIGNMENTS

TEACHER NOTES

LEVEL 2 LESSON PLAN

Teacher's Name _____ Date_____

Class(es) _____ Date(s) _____ M Tu W Th F

LOCAL OBJECTIVES	**BRR:** Bell Ringer Review **TWE:** Teacher's Wraparound Edition **CQ:** Chapter Quizzes	**STM:** Student Tape Manual **WKBK:** Workbook
	HOMEWORK ASSIGNMENTS	**TEACHER NOTES**

Teacher's Name _____ Date _____

Class(es) _____ Date(s) _____ M Tu W Th F

LOCAL OBJECTIVES	**BRR:** Bell Ringer Review	**STM:** Student Tape Manual
	TWE: Teacher's Wraparound Edition	**WKBK:** Workbook
	CQ: Chapter Quizzes	

| | **HOMEWORK ASSIGNMENTS** | **TEACHER NOTES** |

Teacher's Name _____ Date _____

Class(es) _____ Date(s) _____ M Tu W Th F

LOCAL OBJECTIVES	**BRR:** Bell Ringer Review **STM:** Student Tape Manual
	TWE: Teacher's Wraparound Edition **WKBK:** Workbook
	CQ: Chapter Quizzes

	HOMEWORK ASSIGNMENTS	**TEACHER NOTES**

Teacher's Name _____ Date _____

Class(es) _____ Date(s) _____ M Tu W Th F

LOCAL OBJECTIVES	**BRR:** Bell Ringer Review **STM:** Student Tape Manual **TWE:** Teacher's Wraparound Edition **WKBK:** Workbook **CQ:** Chapter Quizzes

HOMEWORK ASSIGNMENTS   **TEACHER NOTES**

Teacher's Name _____ Date _____

Class(es) _____ Date(s) _____ M Tu W Th F

LOCAL OBJECTIVES	**BRR:** Bell Ringer Review **TWE:** Teacher's Wraparound Edition **CQ:** Chapter Quizzes	**STM:** Student Tape Manual **WKBK:** Workbook

HOMEWORK ASSIGNMENTS   **TEACHER NOTES**

¡Buen viaje! LEVEL 2 LESSON PLAN

Teacher's Name _____ Date _____

Class(es) _____ Date(s) _____ M Tu W Th F

LOCAL OBJECTIVES	**BRR:** Bell Ringer Review **TWE:** Teacher's Wraparound Edition **CQ:** Chapter Quizzes	**STM:** Student Tape Manual **WKBK:** Workbook

	HOMEWORK ASSIGNMENTS	TEACHER NOTES

LEVEL 2 LESSON PLAN

Teacher's Name _____ Date _____

Class(es) _____ Date(s) _____ M Tu W Th F

LOCAL OBJECTIVES	BRR: Bell Ringer Review TWE: Teacher's Wraparound Edition CQ: Chapter Quizzes	STM: Student Tape Manual WKBK: Workbook
	HOMEWORK ASSIGNMENTS	TEACHER NOTES

Teacher's Name _____ Date _____

Class(es) _____ Date(s) _____ M Tu W Th F

LOCAL OBJECTIVES	**BRR:** Bell Ringer Review	**STM:** Student Tape Manual
	TWE: Teacher's Wraparound Edition	**WKBK:** Workbook
	CQ: Chapter Quizzes	

HOMEWORK ASSIGNMENTS

TEACHER NOTES